William Henry Rideing

A-saddle in the wild West

A glimpse of travel among the mountains, lava beds sand deserts

William Henry Rideing

A-saddle in the wild West

A glimpse of travel among the mountains, lava beds sand deserts

ISBN/EAN: 9783337210991

Printed in Europe, USA, Canada, Australia, Japan

Cover: Foto ©Andreas Hilbeck / pixelio.de

More available books at **www.hansebooks.com**

APPLETONS' NEW HANDY-VOLUME SERIES.

A-SADDLE

IN THE

WILD WEST.

A GLIMPSE OF TRAVEL

AMONG THE

MOUNTAINS, LAVA BEDS, SAND DESERTS, ADOBE TOWNS, INDIAN RESERVATIONS, AND ANCIENT PUEBLOS OF SOUTHERN COLORADO, NEW MEXICO, AND ARIZONA.

BY

WILLIAM H. RIDEING,

ATTACHED TO THE GEOGRAPHICAL SURVEYS AND EXPLORATIONS WEST OF THE ONE HUNDREDTH MERIDIAN IN CHARGE OF LIEUTENANT GEORGE M. WHEELER, DURING THE FIELD SEASONS OF 1875 AND 1876.

NEW YORK:
D. APPLETON AND COMPANY.
549 & 551 BROADWAY.
1879.

PREFACE.

THE geographical and geological surveys and explorations conducted with so much spirit by the expeditions under Lieutenant George M. Wheeler during the past eight or nine years, have shown that, however familiar the sections penetrated by the Pacific Railways and their branches are, vast tracts of country remain to absorb the attention of the geographer for many years to come. Each field season discovers some new area interesting on account of its zoölogy, its geology, its picturesqueness, or all those things combined ; and the value of the resultant contributions to science has been widely recognized. In the modest way of a newspaper correspondent, the writer shared the opportunities of the expedition in charge of Lieutenant Wheeler during two years, and traveled some four thousand miles a-saddle in New

Mexico, Arizona, Southern Colorado, Nevada, and Eastern California. His contribution, offered in this volume, is devoted not to technicalities, but to the elucidation of the picturesque elements of the country traversed and the amusing features of rough camp life. Parts of it have appeared in various magazines and newspapers, but the whole has been rewritten, condensed, and revised. A word should be added in recognition of the excellence of the work done by Lieutenant Wheeler's surveys, and the exceptional economy with which they have been conducted.

CONTENTS.

PAGE

CHAPTER I.
A GREENHORN IN CAMP.

A First Glimpse of the Rocky Mountains—The Frugality of an Explorer's Mess—Looking for Rattlesnakes—The Routine of a Day—A Fable about Prairie-Dogs—Travelers on the Colorado Highways—A Wind-Storm on Apache Creek—Over the Sangré del Cristo Pass . 9

CHAPTER II.
LIFE AT A FRONTIER POST.

The Delusive Pleasures of a Camp Fire—Reminiscences of the Negro Cook—A Modern Nick of the Woods—Peculiarities of a Sage-Bush Desert—Our Arrival at Fort Garland—The Exigencies of Military Life on the Frontier—The Adventures of a German Recruit—Some Millionaires of the Future 22

CHAPTER III.
THE MEXICANS OF THE SOUTHWESTERN TERRITORIES.

Characteristics of Sierra Blanca and Baldy Peak—The Plazas of Conejos—A Polite Alcalde—Adobe Architecture—An Unfavorable View of El Gringo—The Superstitious Rites of the Penitentes—A Modern Crucifixion—The Melodious Voices of the Señoritas . 35

CHAPTER IV.

AN UNBEATEN TRAIL.

The Luxuriant Vegetation of the Conejos Cañon—Sleeping under Ice in June—The Cañon of Los Piños—The Head Waters of the Rio Chama—The Sublimity of Night in the Mountains—Sam Abbey's Encounter with the Cinnamon Bear—The Coyotes' Serenade . 49

CHAPTER V.

MOUNTAINEERING IN THE SAN JUAN RANGE.

A Difficult March—The Startling Features of a Mountain Marsh—Our Topographer's Deer—A Camp in Utter Solitude—Adventure as a Monomania—The Snow Flowers of an Alpine Lake—On the Top of Banded Peak—Two Hundred Miles at a Glance—Mr. Clark's Peril—Head First Down a Cañon 65

CHAPTER VI.

ISSUE DAY AT AN INDIAN AGENCY.

The Trader's Store at Tierra Amarilla—A Gathering of Utes, Navajos, and Apaches—The Subordination of Women—The Beauty of the Young Squaws—How Arrows are Poisoned—The Tribulations of an Indian Agent 79

CHAPTER VII.

THE MIRACULOUS MESA COUNTRY.

A Prospect of Suffering—A Counterpart of the Yellowstone—The Cities Wrought by Rain—On the Summit of the Continental Divide—The Rock Fantasies of the Cañon Blanco—A Region without Water and without Vegetation—The Extinct Races of New Mexico and their Ruins—The Wonders of Pueblo Pintado . 86

CONTENTS.

CHAPTER VIII.
OVER THE CHASKA MOUNTAINS TO FORT WINGATE.
PAGE
Out of the Desert into a Paradise—The Navajo Reservation—The Amicability of the Tribe—An Old Chief's Idea of Whisky—The Giant's Armchair—Concerning several Interesting Members of the Camp—An Adventure at Albuquerque 101

CHAPTER IX.
A COUNTRY FOR COLONIZATION.
A Geological Supper—What a Young Man might do in the Zuñi Mountains—Sheep-Farming in New Mexico—A Narrow Escape from Drowning in a Mud Spring—Emigrants from Indiana—All Night in a Mexican Ranch 113

CHAPTER X.
A MODERN PUEBLO.
Peeping into a Crater—The Wonders at the Bottom—Traveling over a Lava Bed—The Settlement of Laguna—The Dress and Personal Appearance of the Pueblo Indians—Madame Pueblo—Old Palestine Reproduced—A Pastoral Community—The Pharisaism of the Missionaries—The Chasm in the Plain—The Fertility of the Bottom Lands of the Rio Grande . 124

CHAPTER XI.
SANTA FÉ.
The Capital of New Mexico—The Modesty of the Señoras—The Appearance of the Streets—A Very Mixed Population—The Attractions of a Baby Carriage—Croquet in the Mountains—Scenes around a Gambling

Table—The Great Army Game of "Chuck-a-Luck"—
A Mexican Ball 139

CHAPTER XII.
A SPECIAL CORRESPONDENT INVALIDED.

The Dangers of the Arroyas—An Unusual Telegraph Line
—A Church Three Centuries Old—The Sanguinary
Feuds of the Mexicans and Indians—An Attack of
Mountain Fever—Sixty Miles for Medicine . . 147

CHAPTER XIII.
AN EVENTFUL STAGE-COACH JOURNEY.

Primitive Agriculture—How the Writer "Fixed" the Conductor—Three Texan Stockmen on a Carouse—The
Beauties of Fisher's Peak — The Expedition seen
through the Smoke of a Cigar 156

A-SADDLE IN THE WILD WEST.

CHAPTER I.

A GREENHORN IN CAMP.

A First Glimpse of the Rocky Mountains—The Frugality of an Explorer's Mess—Looking for Rattlesnakes—The Routine of a Day—A Fable about Prairie-Dogs.—Travelers on the Colorado Highways—A Wind-Storm on Apache Creek—Over the Sangré del Cristo Pass.

WHETHER it is attended by expectations of pleasure or apprehensions of discomfort, the uncertainty which unfolds the future is often more disturbing than the least auspicious of actual experiences ; and when three years ago I left New York to join the Geographical Survey under Lieutenant George M. Wheeler, not a little uneasiness moderated my anticipations of the pleasure to be derived from the coming events. On the fourth day the Rocky Mountains became visible—a hazy succession of curves, accentuated by many peaks and streaked with the whitest of white snow, which seemed to be undergoing evaporation; and on the fifth day, after a night in Denver, I entered the organizing camp on the outskirts of Pueblo, Southern Colorado. It was all strange and discomforting—a new experience of scenery and life to me. The rarefied air had parched and cracked my lips; my skin and clothing had acquired the texture of sand-paper; my eyes blinked in the brazen light. We had left the East in the soft, humid greenness of early May, and that seemed very distant and desirable now. The soil was loose to a depth of two or three inches, and a breath of wind was sufficient to whirl it into the upper space. The little grass and foliage visible were parched. In places the soil was split with thirsty veins as though it would open and fall apart, forming another of the frequent vertical-walled gullies which the wash of the rain had made. The superabundant sage-bushes spread their knotted and fibrous branches in every direction, until the distance seemed to fade away in the pallor of their heavy leaves. The little town was shut in by *mesas*, which had the appearance of artificial embankments newly made. The Arkansas, flowing muddily and frothily, had forced an edge of verdure along its shores, and Pike's Peak and its neighbors in the west were gathering deepening purple and gold from the approaching blaze of sunset.

In a grove of cottonwoods outside the town

the tents of the expedition were pitched in a hollow square, and I entered camp with the melancholy sense of isolation and strangeness which a boy might feel in first leaving home, or a traveler in alighting in a country the language and people of which were altogether unfamiliar to him. The experience was not only new, but altogether different from what I had anticipated. Speaking vernacularly, I was a "fresh"; literally, wholly unversed in camp life. The expedition had a military basis, but no uniform was visible among the men who were adjusting barometers, aneroids, thermometers, hygrometers, and theodolites, nor among those who were seated in their tents writing or furbishing rifles and filling cartridge shells. Whatever social or military distinction some of the members of the camp possessed was hidden in a democratic simplicity of dress. A blue or gray flannel shirt, a pair of buckskin trousers, a soft felt hat, and a pistol-belt with a bowie knife ensheathed, made up the prevalent costume ; and this was modified in some instances by a straw hat or a pith helmet. I was shown to a tent which was to be mine. I had expected a spacious four-walled one, but this pointed out to me was three feet high, five feet long, and four feet wide—a piece of canvas supported by a guy rope and two sticks. Silently and patiently I crawled in and changed my ordinary clothing for a handsome and elaborate shooting suit made for me by a New York tailor. As I emerged, this foppery seemed too obvious in contrast with the simple dress of the others, and I left the coat and vest behind; but still I was not comfortable.

Three divisions of the survey, each composed of ten men, formed the camp, and at three corners of the hollow square the cooks were preparing the separate messes over wood-fires. An oil-cloth was spread on the ground, and small spaces were partitioned off by tin cups and blackish knives and forks. The cook then placed several tin vessels, containing sugar, coffee, bacon, and hot bread, between the other utensils. A wind was blowing, and the bacon and bread were covered with dust to the depth of a quarter of an inch before the men in buckskin had responded to the cook's tattoo beaten on one of his pans. They squatted or lay at three-quarters length opposite the plates, helped themselves to the bacon, and, after scraping the dust off, appeared to enjoy it. A bulky person, with a brusque manner and a particularly large appetite, rested on his elbows at one end of the cloth. While I was contemplating the barbarian informality of the meal a personal acquaintance approached me. "When will the officers' mess be served?" I innocently asked. He could not conceal his smile. "Officers and men mess together, my dear fellow—this is ours," he said, indicating the oil-cloth and the now incrusted bacon. "Bless my soul! I've neglected to introduce you!" he added, and forthwith he presented me to the bulky gentleman, who was Lieutenant Marshall, the officer in general charge of the Colorado section of the expedition. I essayed eating a small piece of the bacon, but it was as unpalatable as sand-paper; and then I climbed one of the surrounding hills to see the sun touch all the mountains with fire for a moment before leaving them dark and vivid against a steel-gray sky.

The first night spent in the open air by a person habituated to city life can not be very tranquil to him, especially if it is in a country where rattlesnakes and centipedes abound. It seemed as if a myriad of grasshoppers had taken possession of my bed, and it was with difficulty that I could be assured that they were not more deadly insects, as they crawled over me and alighted on my face. During the night the wind increased, and my tent collapsed over me. "Never mind; lie as you are till morning," said my experienced acquaintance. Ah, how I envied the nonchalance with which he took everything! And while I waited for morning, the wind ceased and a heavy rain began to fall. That I lay in a mud-puddle amid soaked blankets at daybreak was a secondary consideration. My first thought was for rattlesnakes, and I took each boot with extreme care and shook it to expel any viper that might have selected it for refuge during the night. I also turned the blankets over in quest of similar enemies, and then dressed. The idea of dressing in a fine, compact, searching rain, with a chilling wind blowing at the same time! "It's very imprudent," I said to the acquaintance before mentioned, who was a veteran surveyor. "It's quite uninjurious," he answered; and as the cook's tattoo was heard he added, "Come to breakfast." There was the same oil-cloth on the ground, and the same bacon on the blackish tin plates. But I was more reconciled than at supper time, and in a few days I began to feel at home.

In the course of a week the three divisions of the survey took the field, each being composed of an officer in charge, a topographer, an odometer recorder, a meteorologist, a geologist, a cook, and three packers. We separated from the two other parties, not expecting to meet them again until the end of the season, six months later, and then we entered on the campaign.

One little episode repeated itself from day to day. It never missed; it was inevitable. No matter where we happened to be, or what the weather was, a deep-throated voice was heard in camp before sunrise every morning, calling, "Five o'clock! Turn out." The sleepers rolled over in their blankets, sighed and yawned, and longed to resign themselves to sleep again; but the command was imperative. Perhaps we had pitched our little tents on the slope of a cañon; the air was frosty, and puffs of gray clouds were drifting above the walls of rock and pines. The cook was already up, and was bending over his fire with a "sizzling" panful of bacon. "Now, boys, ten minutes past five!" The weary ones rolled over and stretched themselves once more, and several pairs of legs were seen backing out of the tents. "Ugh! How cold the morning is!" "Did you hear the coyotes last night?" "Hear them? Confound them! I couldn't close my eyes for them!" Such questions were asked and answered with chattering teeth while the brown-faced fellows who had just turned out stood irresolutely near their tents. But it was only for a moment. There was a search for towels, sponges, and soap boxes. Under the brush at one side of the cañon was a noisy brooklet of melted snow. Into this half a dozen heads were quickly dipped, and when they came out they were as fresh and bright as the blue sky that was revealed as the clouds drifted away. The big sponges became little cataracts, and the soap was used with a degree of lavishness that produced enough lather to obscure the little stream as it flowed swiftly by the camp.

When the splashing was done breakfast was served. There was some very fat bacon, boiled rice, beans, and bread—no butter nor milk; but these coarse things were consumed with as much relish as the choicest meats, and the platters were emptied and filled again and again. The officers of the expedition and the laborers sat side by side. All ceremonies were omitted. The eating was done quickly and heartily, and by half-past five o'clock the cook had "the table" cleared. Next the tents were pulled down and rolled up. The foundation of each man's bed was a strip of canvas as broad and as long as the tent, and above this he had a rubber blanket, on which two or three pairs of woolen blankets were stretched; not the softest or warmest kind of a couch, but, when the ground did not bristle with rocks, it was astonishing how soundly one could sleep upon it. By twenty minutes to six all the bedding had been rolled into marvelously compact bundles—each man, from the lieutenant to the cook, having done his own share of the work— and the packers had begun to load the mules. The reader probably understands that a party of ten men traveling in an uninhabited country on a scientific expedition must have considerable baggage with them even when everything superfluous is excluded. There were the instruments, the record books, and the provisions, of which we were often compelled to carry enough for thirty days at a time. He will also probably understand that, as our road sometimes lay up the sides of precipitous cliffs and down mountain trails, it was impossible for us to use wagons. We put our faith in a pack-train composed of mules, each carrying a separate load on a pack-saddle or *apparajo*. "Do you know how to pack a mule?" some one once asked a small boy in Arizona. "You bet!" he answered sweetly, with childish confidence. "*Cinch* him plenty tight, and then cry 'Bueno'"—*cinch* meaning the girth and *bueno* meaning good. But packing a mule is not such an easy task, and to do it well requires all the skill of a man trained to the business. The *apparajo* is a sort of peaked saddle made of leather and stuffed with hay. It is firmly strapped on to the animal, which often shows decided objections to the strain by throwing itself several feet into the air and waving its legs with such velocity that the four seem to be four hundred. The nimblest gymnast that ever twisted himself into miraculous shapelessness could not excel the contortions of a wild mule. He—the mule—flings himself about with the resilience of an India-rubber ball; expands himself to the size of a small elephant, and the next moment compresses himself into half his natural proportions. No feat of agility is impossible to him. But the experienced packer looks upon his wildest tricks as at the antics of a mere baby, and leads him to the point of duty at a rope's end in a cool and daring way that subdues his angry passions in a moment.

Before seven o'clock we were on the road, and our marches were usually about twenty miles a day, although they occasionally covered between thirty and forty miles when it was necessary to force them for water. We went southward from Pueblo over the mountain by the Sangré del Cristo Pass to Fort Garland. The first days were not pleasant to the greenhorn. The yellow dust was insufferable and insinuating; we felt more than ever like sand-paper. A chain of dark purple peaks broke the western horizon. Far behind and before us were desolate reaches of land, parched and fallow. The only signs of verdure were in the bunches of sparse grass, set about six inches apart, and the hoary cactus with its pretty yellow flowers. We did not see a tree in many miles, nor other shrub than the scrubby little sage-bushes, which are abundant enough. The animal life of the region was also limited. No birds were audible; a moccasin snake hid itself under a sage-bush, or a swift darted into its retreat, and a few prairie dogs barked at us in the squeaking treble of a talking doll. There is a tradition that the prairie dog, the owl, and the rattlesnake live peaceably together in one dwelling, but all plainsmen deride the idea. The owl is sometimes found perched on a bush near the prairie dog's house, watching intently for the inmate to come out, and the rattlesnake also casts a longing eye on the same spot; but neither the owl nor the rattlesnake is actuated by any desire to be sociable. The rattlesnake is of the opinion, as a plainsman said, that "prairie dog's mighty nice eatin'."

But there was traffic on the road, and the monotony was not so great as when, later in the season, we followed an old trail or made a new one in a country that is not penetrated by white men once in a score of years. We occasionally passed a train of wagons with emigrants from Missouri, who were seeking new homes in the West. The cattle followed behind and the children ran on before, careless of heat, dust, and thirst. The sunburnt men strode along in great high boots, smoking and chatting, and the women sat in the wagons. At sundown they encamped near a pool or brook, and by sunrise next morning were on the road again, restless until the end of their long journey. Ascending a hill, we heard a report like that of a rifle, and when we attained the crest saw a Mexican bull team coming up the other slope, driven by dark-eyed, oval-faced Pueblo Indians, who execrated the animals in execrable Spanish. Their wagons were loaded with wool consigned to the East, and the report was produced by a dexterous swing of their long rawhide whips. The most frequent wayfarers were the freighters, who hire themselves and their teams for the conveyance of merchandise from point to point, their journeys sometimes occupying three or four months. At night the solitary freighter unharnesses his animals and pickets them out to graze, afterward cooking and eating his lonely supper. He goes to sleep with his hand on his revolver, and the least unusual sound awakens him and his dogs.

At the end of the second day's march we encamped by Apache Creek, near two deserted ranches from which the occupants had flown in sheer despair. When we arrived the evening was calm, cloudless, and without any indications of a storm; but in less than ten minutes the mountains were seemingly enshrouded in a gray rainy vapor. As the packers were covering the boxes, the wind swept down upon us with the impetuosity and force of a cyclone, increasing in violence every moment until our tents were all upset. This was not the worst. The gale carried not rain but dense clouds of dust with it, that filled our ears, mouth, and eyes; dressing-cases, mess-chests, clothes-bags, and bedding. Lieutenant Morrison, of the Sixth Cavalry, our officer in charge, and Mr. Clark, the topographer, took possession of one of the deserted ranches, and vainly endeavored to fill a barometer tube with mercury. They worked patiently until after midnight, and then, after all their painstaking, a sudden gust of wind cracked and broke the slender glass. Meanwhile we lay under our tents on a ridge of black sand, and felt superlatively disconsolate.

From Apache Creek we went southward along the eastern foot-hills of the mountains to Badito.

We passed the Huerfano, an isolated peak projected above the green sea of the prairie, and thence traveled over the Sangré del Cristo. The Wet Mountains came into view, and the verdure became more abundant and more varied in shade. Tall pines cast their long shadows on the slopes, and moaned as the increasing wind stirred among their straight and dusky branches. Now and then an alpine bluebell nodded at us or a wild rose peeped out of a thicket. The valleys lay under a dense growth of shrubbery, as leafy and as lustrous as the arbor vitæ. We toiled over the innumerable foothills—the lowest loftier than Mount Washington—and far away could see the snowy spires and domes of the Sierra Blanca, and the smooth, precipitous gray walls of Baldy Peak. No sooner had we attained the crest of one hill than another still higher appeared, and our outlook expanded every minute. We followed the trail through a deep grove, and glanced down through a natural clearing in the pines and aspens on ninety miles of country, in which the distant mountains looked like islands in a wide ocean. The life limits were not far above, and the wind roared among the trees with the sound of a tremendous cataract. Whole forests of pines were prone on the slopes, torn from their beds by the previous winter's tempests. At last it seemed that we had reached the sky itself and were set in a zone of frosty azure. Our path was like an opening seam in the side of the mountain. We climbed over fallen logs and bowlders, and after a six hours' march stood upon the summit of the Sangré del Cristo.

That night our tents were pitched in a cañon to the southwest of the mountain. Gloomy forests of pine locked us in, and rugged masses of cloud drifted overhead. The cold was intense, although the day had been very hot, and the flapping of our tents reminded us of a boisterous night at sea.

CHAPTER II.

LIFE AT A FRONTIER POST.

The Delusive Pleasures of a Camp Fire—Reminiscences of the Negro Cook—A Modern Nick of the Woods—Peculiarities of a Sage-Bush Desert—Our Arrival at Fort Garland—The Exigencies of Military Life on the Frontier—The Adventures of a German Recruit—Some Millionaires of the Future.

ONE of the many pleasures which inexperienced people insist upon attributing to out-door life is the camp fire. The greenhorn was fond of watching the smoke winding upward awhile, and then losing itself in the illimitable—the flicker and glow on the men crowding near the blaze, that, with a sudden flash, lighted a single face for a moment and brought all the features into distinctness, and then obliterated them with a shadow. But the picturesque and comfort are qualities that do not always go together; and while the camp fire is all very well for those who are content with the prettiness of its tongues of flame and breath of sparks, it is practically a nuisance. It always reminded the greenhorn of how cold his back was. Those who were allured to it were (nearly) roasted to death on one side and (nearly) frozen to death on the other. The smoke was suffocating, the flame scorching, and the flying sparks raised serious blisters on the exposed parts of the skin. Our lungs labored under the astringency of the fumes that found their way into them. As a matter of fact, the pleasures of the camp fire exist largely in the imagination; but to be fair, its glow drove some of the oppression away from our isolated halting places. When supper was over and our pipes were lighted—the delicate meerschaum upon which its owner lavished inordinate care, the substantial briers, and the cook's odoriferous cutty with a piece of dough inserted in a calamitous breech of the bowl—yarns were busily spun, and the brighter the blaze was the more exciting were the stories told. Lieutenant Morrison was usually absent from these gatherings of wonder-mongers, and could be found stretched out on a blanket star-gazing with a quadrant, and absorbed in the astronomical observations which form an important part of the work of the survey. The scientific men, being young and diffident, could only be heard in an occasional interrogation, and the burden of narrative fell upon the packers and cook, who had no end of material to sustain it. Alick had come to Colorado during the Pike's Peak excitement, and had since led a wild life, stock-raising in Texas and prospecting for gold among the mountains, from Harney's Peak in the Black Hills down to the spurs of the San Juan; Sam had fought through the war, and coming out unscathed had since been trying to dispose of himself among the ruffianly free-shooters of border towns; Nick had passed a good part of his young life buffalo-hunting on the plains; and Green Terrill, the cook, could boast that he "never had enough liquor aboard to make him walk unsteady, and never took the good Lord Almighty's name in vain in all his life"—which is a great deal more than most men who have spent fifteen years in Colorado and Nevada can veraciously say for themselves. The episodes in the lives of these waifs—the patient industry of the gold-seeker, the nerve and daring of the huntsman, the ingenuity of the scout, and the recklessness of the frontiersman—afforded the topics; and when the resinous pine logs sang and the flames leaped to their highest, our pulses beat faster as we listened to the strange stories told. The cook's inexhaustible theme was old times in Denver and intercourse with the Indians on Bitter Creek. He had no faith in the noble savage ; and when a humorous Navajo playfully pulled his bow on him, Green quickly and seriously cocked his carbine, and the Indian only saved his life by the most earnest gesticulations of amity and innocence.

"You bet I ain't goin' to take no stock in dem fellows," said Green. " Seed too much of dem fur dat. Way up on Bitter Creek some of dem dogorned Sioux was playin' wild, an' Tom Belcher, what's got a big ranch dare, comes to me and says to me if I didn't want to herd his cattle for him. 'Well,' I says, 'I didn't mind,' and he offered me *free* dollars for de night. It was jist about *dust* when I went out into de field where dem cattle was, and dare was a big tame steeah wat day called Tommy, dat was jist so quiet dat you could lay down beside him. I ain't no fool now ; so, thinks I, if dare war any of dem fell's about I'd wait an' see ; an' I laid me down by Tommy, dat was a kind of barricade, you know, an' kep one eye open. James River ! "—this was one of the few harmless expletives that Green occasionally let off—" James River ! Fust one fell' leaped out of de bush ; den another, soh, James River ! until dare was six, all scrapin' an' whoopin' an' swingin' roun' like a pack of mad wolves. Well, I jest got up an' got, and says to Tom Belcher when I got to de ranch, 'Guess I don't want no free doll's,' says I. 'What's de matter?' says he ; 'seed any Injins?' 'Yes,' says I. 'Well, dey didn't hurt you,' says he. 'No,' says I, 'and thank the good Lord for it!' Eh?" [A long pause.] "What?" [Another pause.] "You bet!" [A chuckle, ending in a loud laugh in which all the camp joined.]

After a burst of this kind five minutes were allowed for refreshment in the form of contemplative expectoration; and if the coyotes in the neighborhood were well behaved, they assisted with a Wagnerian chorus. But Green was heard at his best in describing old Denver days, when one "gentleman" would often shoot at another "gentleman's" nose simply to see how nearly he could graze it. "Dem was de times, afore de railroad come in. Of course dare warn't no water-works den, jes' a scrapin' of wooden shanties, an' mos' of dem was salooms an' faro shops. Dat's been my ruin, dat faro has. Seen a lot of fellers come down from de mountains with some loose dust, go into Bill H——'s place over de ole variety theatre, an' de game would go on jes' 'bout ten minutes, when de lights would go out, an' shoo! James River! you bet dis hyar ear tingled some. Lord, de shots was jus' abuzzing 'bout like hornicks, an' de chairs an' tables an' glasses were flyin' roun' quite lively now, I jes' tell you! De music stool took me right in de neck, an' I had a sore froat fur free weeks after. Eh? What? You bet! A fellow carried roun' a man's hand de next day, an' showed it too, an' a friend of his'n had another man's nose. Why warn't dey arrested? 'Cause no one ever wanted dem two fell's; dey was too influentium in society. I know now; I've been dare afore de railroad come in. Of course dare wusn't no water-works den, but dare was a heap of money. Jes' a common laborer got his $30 and $40 a week, and cooks got $100 and $125, many and many of 'em. I got $50 myself, and de Boots in de same house never shined a pair of boots in his life for less dan a dollar. Dem was de times afore de railroad come in, an' as soon as dat got dare, labor was cheaper, of course, an' somehow de old high-toned citizens of de place went away."

Green then inquired if the company had heard of Jem Wagener: all the packers knew him quite well, and it turned out that he was a sort of Nick of the Woods, sworn to kill every squaw and papoose at sight in avengement of the murder of his own wife and children by the Indians. Another half hour was occupied by a narrative of his thrilling deeds; and having by this time become sleepy, we retired to our tents for a seven hours' rest.

The afternoon after our passage of the Sangré del Cristo we seemed to be threading our way over a wide field of weather-beaten stubble or a litter of yellow-brown walnut shavings. Not a speck of verdure could be seen, nor a sign of moisture; neither a hedge nor a fence nor a breath of mist. Space and shadow were annihilated. The most distant objects appeared to be within a ten minutes' run, and especially distinct were the low irregular banks of snow that broke upon the acute horizon with painful intensity. The level road of decomposed granite was hot and yellow, and for miles a serpentine cloud of dust floated over our wake.

The field of stubble was an elevated plateau; the walnut shavings were the weazen, death-like sage-bushes; and the banks of snow that seemed to be so near were the Sierra Blanca, the Sangré del Cristo, and other peaks from ten to thirty miles away. Toiling along for another hour, the sun meanwhile beating down upon us with wilting ardor despite our altitude—the atmosphere and earth voiceless and forsaken—we reached a hollow watered by a swift creek, and here our eyes were gratified by the bright verdure of a few cottonwoods and shrubs. Across the low divide that separated this valley from the next we obtained a glimpse of our destination—a rectangular group of adobe buildings, flat-roofed, squat, and altogether dispiriting in their unmitigated ugliness, with the United States flag sultrily clinging to a central pole. This was Fort Garland. In the southwest, forty or fifty miles away, a long row of whitened summits, spurs of the San Juan range, were clouded in the smoke of forest fires; and in the east the main range trended toward the south until its mountains became mere specks to our vision. But the lofty background encircled a horribly unvaried desert, with the same characterizing features, the same absence of fresh colors and attractive forms, as our route of the afternoon. We wondered how a man could look upon it from day to day without yielding to its communicative oppressiveness ; and when we were inside the walls of the fort, we pitied the officers and men condemned to live in so desolate a place.

Military exigencies allow no choice, however, and the army news in the papers records the name of some one ordered to duty in the Department of the Missouri, which probably means to the soldier concerned several years of unproductive, unrewarded, and wholly unsatisfactory service on the wild Western frontier. From Fort Leavenworth, in Kansas, he is ordered to Fort Stanton, in New Mexico ; from Fort Stanton to Fort Fetterman, in Wyoming ; from Fort Fetterman to Fort Lyon, in Colorado ; and from Fort Lyon, perhaps, to Fort Garland. During all this, his activity is restrained in every direction, and he sinks into a plodding, sullen sort of existence, the brightest dream in which is of the limpid rivers and succulent verdure nearer the seaboard. Frontier life suggests a sort of poetic expansiveness to the inexperienced, but to the soldier it involves, except in the case of an Indian war, a career of humdrum routine.

Garland is one of the oldest military establishments in Colorado, and one of the pleasantest, though its red adobe or sun-dried brick buildings are in a state of increasing and unprepossessing dilapidation. At the date of our visit the nearest railroad station was Pueblo, eighty miles northward, and occasional travelers and the semi-weekly mail were the only links between the exiles and the far-distant, familiar world. Nevertheless, not an item of discipline was omitted. The reveillé was beaten at the same moment— allowing for the difference of longitude—that it rumbled over the waters of New York Bay. Guard was mounted and relieved in the fullest and neatest dress, and to inspiriting music, even though six men were all the post could muster. Reports were submitted and received with the same pomp and circumstance as are observed in the largest army, and the sentries challenged with unremitted vigilance all who passed the gates. The only variations to these exacting formalities were when intelligence arrived of Indian depredations, and a company of cavalry was sent out; or when the guard-house was broken and a prisoner escaped. This latter episode was of frequent occurrence. Not a few risked capture and severe punishment for the chance of an escape from the confinement and dull surroundings.

Many recruits are sent out from the East to the West, including some young German immigrants,

who, landing without a knowledge of English and
failing to obtain employment, enlist in order to
learn the language ; for the idioms of which, at
least, the army is doubtless an excellent school.
We met such a one in the person of a young
architect, who when he arrived in New York
could not speak a word of English, and who,
when his little fortune had been reduced to the
total of a few dollars, sought out an enlisting
sergeant, and was accepted. The sergeant took
him to all the beer-gardens in the city, and treated him with the most delicate consideration, allowing him to pay the expenses of both, and as-
suring him, as was evident, that a soldier's life
was an easy one at this rate. But when the last
dollar of his shallow purse had been expended,
he was sent with several others to Governor's
Island, where the petty officers berated him vigorously for misunderstanding their orders. He made
many ludicrous mistakes, of course, and his Eng-
lish-speaking comrades subjected him to all kinds
of practical jokes. All the articles of equipment
supplied for him were stolen, except a pair of
blue trousers, and, as he was determined to save
these, he hid them in one of the cannons. On the
day following some dignitary was either entering or leaving port, and a salute was ordered to
be fired. The men stood at the different guns, and
loaded them, and each went off in succession until
the turn came for the last one. In vain the gun-

ner applied the light to the breech of this, in vain the officers raged, and in vain the completion of the salute was listened for. The thing would not "go off," and, when an investigation was made, the cause became apparent in the recruit's black and greasy trousers. After a few months' probation at Governor's Island, he was ordered to a regiment in New Mexico, and thence from fort to fort until he eventually reached Garland.

There is one pleasant feature about Fort Garland. The log and adobe houses of the *rancheros* do not in the least exceed the Spartan limit of a few chairs, a table, and a chromo in matters of decoration or luxury. But the officers contrive to crowd many significant little evidences of refinement into their incommodious quarters, notwithstanding the difficulty of obtaining anything except the necessaries of life. The rooms are in some instances carpeted with buffalo-robes and bear-skins, while the walls are adorned with guns and relics of the chase. To members of our expedition coming out of the field, this revelation of domesticity and comfort proved a grateful change from the hardships of an American explorers' camp.

A railway now passes through Fort Garland, and a little city has sprung out of the surrounding desert: but four years ago very few strangers found their way there. Occasionally a solitary "prospector" came with all his immediate possessions—a pick-axe, a spade, a rifle, and a bag of provisions—heaped up on the back of a little donkey—his future and greater wealth lying in the gaunt mountains of the San Juan, to which he was bound; some straggling Apaches loitered within the fort for a few hours; a Mexican bull-team plodded by with a heavy load of wool; and a pair of stockmen delayed a moment to try the whisky at the sutler's store before they galloped away to a neighboring ranch. But in addition to the travelers a curious little society of mixed elements gathered about the fort. There was a fresh-colored collegian from Cambridge, England, who had come hither, of all places in the world, to seek his fortune; the agent of a land company; and a mysterious idle vagrant known as the "Major," who was understood to be an ex-Confederate officer. The Major's peculiarity was an odd manner of making a secret of all his communications. He would confide an innocent remark about the mules or weather to us as though it was a key to some enormous conspiracy; and in the same way he would ask us the price of shoe-leather in the lowest and most suspicious of undertones. His knowledge of Washington society was inexhaustible; but this was of little practical benefit to him, as we found that he was working on a ranch for forty dollars a month, and before we left the fort he offered himself to us as a laborer with the pack-train.

Everybody at the fort seemed anxious to get

away; the only exception was the sutler, who was making a fortune. Much of the comfort at a frontier post depends on the character of the sutler's store, and that at Garland was one of the best, including in its stock every imaginable and many unimaginable articles, from Wiltshire hams to Mexican spurs, patent medicines to buffalo robes, stationery to saddles, and ammunition to cosmetics. The customers were also heterogeneous, including the officers and men of the fort, the passing emigrants and Indians, the miners and ranchmen, and some Mexican *señoritas* whose chief weakness was articles of Philadelphia perfumery and Birmingham jewelry.

While we sat on the bench in front of the sutler's store one evening, the old fort was transformed into a very pretty object under the magical influence of the brilliant sunset. The surrounding sandy plain melted into gold, and the mountains were flooded with purple. A pale star rose over the eastern ridge, and while in the west the sky was glowing with gorgeous colors, in the east the light was expiring in a deepening blue. But it is only for a moment in a summer's day that Garland looks inviting; and as we left it to resume our course, we again pitied the men condemned to live the year round in this lonely spot.

CHAPTER III.

THE MEXICANS OF THE SOUTHWESTERN TERRITORIES.

Characteristics of Sierra Blanca and Baldy Peak—The Plazas of Conejos—A Polite Alcalde—Adobe Architecture—An Unfavorable View of El Gringo—The Superstitious Rites of the Penitentes—A Modern Crucifixion—The Melodious Voices of the Señoritas.

SEEN from the plain near Fort Garland, Sierra Blanca and Baldy Peak loom up romantically. The upper ridge of the former is broken into several pinnacles with gentle curves between, and its sides are furrowed with deep hollows steeped in the nebulous haze of the clouds. Baldy is almost a pyramid, with barren walls that end in a sharp point twelve thousand feet high, cloven by transverse fissures, in which glaring masses of snow lie until the middle of June. The farther we retreated from them the nearer they appeared to be; and two days after we left Garland, when they were thirty miles distant, they seemed larger and more distinct than when we were within five miles of their bases. Fifty miles is as a stone's throw, and a person unused to the delusive effects of the atmosphere might readily be induced to attempt a walk of twenty-five miles in ten minutes.

Continuing in a southerly course from Blanca, a range of peaks extends, so uniform in their elevation and shape that it is not easy to realize how high they are. But among them are many that soar eleven thousand feet, and a few that are not far short of thirteen thousand. The eye follows them for nearly twenty miles, finding inexhaustible beauties in their soft outlines, the pine and fir-strewn buttresses, and the strange play of light and shadow that dyes them now a purple, then an unfathomable blue, and, toward morning, a hue like that of an opal held up to the sun. But no one can understand the majesty and wonders of these mountains who has not seen them in a storm, when massive volumes of rolling clouds seem rent asunder by their jagged peaks, and stream down upon them like the flames of a pale phosphorescent fire. Then the prairie reaches before us, a desert of green and yellow, and the foothills are enveloped in mysterious and impenetrable shadows, while the uplands are illuminated by white gleams that bring out their contour with marvelous clearness. As the tumultuous clouds come floating out of the west, they break into vertical streaks and shreds of gray—so unusual in form to one who belongs to the East, that he alternates between transport and amazement. A luminous mist rises from the basins near the peaks as these fleecy waves beat against the pinnacles, and their volume is dispersed. The snows become brilliantly white, and the eye is dimmed and pained, and turns away for relief. The extinct volcanic force that upheaved the divide seems still to exert its influence on the atmosphere, and to wreak itself in the wonderful forms of impalpable vapor.

Southward from Garland two singular dome-like peaks are seen, isolated from all others in the chain. These are the San Antonio and the Ute, both of which are over ten thousand feet high; and to the west the snowy crests of the San Juan range loom massively in the clear air, with a hundred other mountains in between. But our path over the level was unsatisfactory and unlovely, interesting only in the manifold evidences it presented of spent volcanoes and the different geological periods. Here a sandy ridge reminded us of the drift, and a little farther on we came upon a sharp needle of basaltic formation that pointed to fires long since burned out. In places the ground consists of decomposed granite that only needs water to make it fruitful. Farther on huge bowlders of scoria are strewn in every direction, imbedded in the hillside, and lying prone in the middle of plains, where they fell centuries ago, fresh from seething craters. A coyote sneaked away at our approach, and an antelope bounded into a thicket. The chattering bark of the impudent little prairie dogs was heard almost incessantly, and their bristling tails were seen whisking above their mounds. The road dwindled into an indistinct trail, and Lieutenant Morrison rode forward, bending over his horse's head, to pick out the obliterated footprints of some hunter or Indian trader who had traveled our way before. About midday the men brought pieces of bread out of their saddle-bags and ate a frugal lunch. Then, when the sun was on the night side of the zenith, we sighted a line of green in the distance which indicated water, and after a hot and dusty march of nine or ten hours, we encamped for the night on the banks of a rapid little mountain stream.

Our second camp after leaving Garland was on the San Antonio River, and thence we went to Conejos in search of a Mexican guide, to show us the best route over the mountains to Tierra Amarilla. Like all the important New Mexican towns, Conejos is subdivided into several villages or plazas a mile or so apart, each consisting of about a dozen adobe dwellings, built irregularly over a small area, without separate inclosures. The Mexican of the Southwestern territories is not extravagant in matters of architecture. He is not the man by temperament or inclination to quarry stone and shape it for a shelter, when lighter material can be found; and his chief aim in constructing his dwelling has apparently been to succeed with as little labor as possible. His feeble indolence was not likely to express itself in such robust edifices of rock as some of the hardier Indians have left on the cliffs to commemorate their former greatness. Had the sun always shone and the winds blown steadily from the south, he would not have built at all; but favorable as the climate is, an occasional tornado in summer and the snows of winter made the erection of a house a painfully unavoidable necessity. Nature accommodated him, however, and, whichever site he chose, he had to go no farther than the spot on which he stood for building materials. The earth only needed mixing with a little water and straw to make it adobe. Adobe, in point of fact, is mud, and by spreading it while it is moist over a rude inclosure of logs, or shaping in into bricks, it can be fashioned without much labor or design into a passably comfortable habitation. This was all that was necessary, and this was all that was done.

If anything is calculated to make a traveler feel homesick, it is a collection of these adobe houses. The prairie-dog throws up a mound around his dwelling; shapeliness and purpose are visible in the nomadic Indian's wigwam; the bamboo house of the South Sea islander has its overlapping roof of palms; but the home of the New Mexican is a cheerless one-storied rectangle, as unpicturesque as an empty soap box, without chimneys, gables, or eaves—four flat, expressionless walls covered in by a flat unmeaning lid, without a curve or projection of any kind to relieve the dead-weight of monotony. Neither mold nor creeper touches it ; age leaves no mark of its caresses upon it, except, perhaps, an unseemly gap here and there, where a portion of the adobe has fallen away. The door has no panels, the window no frame. Barren surfaces meet the eye everywhere, not one sign of beauty or strength ; and the crevices are infested by swarms of lizards, beetles, and hornets, to say nothing of occasional tarantulas, scorpions, and rattlesnakes.

The interior matches the exterior in its prisonlike, angular appearance. The two or three square apartments into which it is divided consist of adobe walls, floors, and ceilings, furnished with a small table, a few kitchen utensils, and a roll of bedding. They have the one merit of being warm in winter and cool in summer ; and it would be unfair to overlook their extreme cleanliness, for however filthy a Mexican woman may be personally, she invariably keeps a clean house, and is never done scrubbing and whitewashing.

Yet, poverty-stricken and destitute of other decorations as these rude houses are, the poorest of them can usually boast of a bit of religious finery ; and though a chair or a table is not included in the furniture, a crucifix dangles over the hearth, and a gaudy Nassau Street print of the Last Supper, the manger of Bethlehem, or the Madonna and Child may be found hanging against the wall.

Lieutenant Morrison and the writer visited the principal plaza together. On our way we accosted a small boy for directions. Doffing his hat, he pointed to a building much larger than the others, which he said was the residence of the alcalde. The New Mexican is usually suave, and this small boy, whose felt hat had lost its brim, and whose ragged trousers were suspended over the shoulders by a string, saluted us with the grave courtesy of a gentleman, scratching himself the while with a furtive vigor that was both amusing and suspicious. But the alcalde—in which country shall we find one more smooth, dignified, and hospitable than he? When he had demonstrated our way to us in voluble Spanish and by earnest gestures, he invited us to dismount and take a cup of coffee or a glass of wine. He was the magistrate of the town, at once the mayor, the police justice, and the town council—as comprehensive a character as the survivor in Gilbert's ballad of "The Nancy Bell." His house was a castle of its kind, and had been built when Indians were troublesome on the border. All the windows looked out upon an interior courtyard, and the door was wide and strong. A look of disappointment passed over the reverend señor's brown face because we declined his hospitalities, and as we left him he reiterated his directions in his anxiety lest we should mistake them. But all New Mexicans are not as agreeable as this one was, as the reader will presently see.

New Mexico, Arizona, and Southern Colorado present the anomalous spectacle of a population alien in blood, language, faith, and customs from the government in the election of which it participates. When the former territory was annexed to the United States by the treaty of Guadalupe Hidalgo in 1848, sixty thousand impoverished and ignorant people were made citizens. They remain impoverished, ignorant, and unassimilated to-day. The preponderating lower classes are in a state of peonage, thriftless and illiterate: a few wealthy persons control the trade of the territory, and a few astute Americans have a complete hold of the politics. More than fifty-two per cent. of the population can neither speak English, nor read nor write any language. Most of the members of the House of Representatives can only read and write Spanish, which is the language of the courts and church. In conversation a *patois* is used which bears about the same degree of relationship to the mother-tongue that the dialect of the Canadian *habitant* bears to Parisian French.

In faith the people are simple, obedient, miracle-loving believers in the most authoritative and absolute Roman Catholicism. Previous to the acquisition of the territory by the United States, their nearest bishop lived over a thousand miles away in old Mexico, and seldom if ever visited so remote a diocese as this. The priests exercised temporal and spiritual powers in the several parishes, and were indescribably corrupt in the use of those powers for their personal benefit and the shameless satisfaction of their lusts. Never was religion further perverted. It became the mere mask of license, and its ministers the priests, not of Christ, but of lechery and greed. At the time when the present archbishop was appointed, he could not close his eyes to the condition of affairs, and summarily dismissed a large number of priests for open immorality; but despite his efforts, which have been sincere and zealous, the Church is still represented in many distant settlements by men who are a disgrace and danger not only to Christianity, but to manhood and freedom. The bishop is a native of France, and most of those under him are French Jesuits, who, while they are not guilty of downright corruption, have not proved themselves in the history of their order the safest guardians of an ignorant people.

The smallest settlements include a church, and whenever the Mexican has risen from the architectural squalor of his squat adobes, his efforts to attain a higher standard have been spent on the edifice that proclaims itself in the cross. In the most distant and impoverished villages a little sanctuary is found, raising its head a few feet above the huts around it, and presenting in its belfry and cornice the only attempt at ornamentation visible. The poverty within is almost pathetic. The bare mud walls are not more than twelve or fifteen feet high, and two small windows admit a drowsy yellow light into the dusty interior. The altar is adorned with cheap engravings, cheap paper flowers, cheap plaster images, cheap tallow candles, and cheap paper lace. It looks like a toy-shop window in firework times. The beams in the ceiling are as rough as the woodman's axe left them. No chairs or seats are provided, and the congregation crouch, Indian fashion, on the hard mud floor. In the larger towns, which are supplied with a resident priest, the church bell is never done ringing for services; but in the far-off districts a wandering padre trots into town some Sunday morning and out of town on Monday morning, not to appear again for three weeks or a month.

The extraordinary credulity and fanaticism of the people are seen in the strongest light, however, during Holy Week, when large numbers throughout the territory participate in the exercises of the Society of Penitentes, which is discountenanced by the priests, though it originally sprang from the Church. The headquarters of this organization are at Mora, and its branches extend in every direction, including among its members a considerable part of the population, both male and female. It meets in the Morada, or assembly hall, and its transactions are secret, but its avowed object is the expiation of sin by the infliction of violent bodily punishment. Toward Good Friday there is an unusual activity in the society, and the town hall is occupied nearly every evening by meetings, which are signalized to the outsiders by dismal cries, groans, and the mysterious rattling of chains—preparations which result on Holy Thursday in the public scourging of those members who desire to chasten themselves and make atonement for their offenses. The day is regarded as a festival, and a crowd of eager spectators gather about the hall. After many preliminary ceremonies, the door is thrown open, and the *penitentes* file into the April twilight of the snow-covered street to the doleful music of a shrill reed instrument played by an attendant. They are destitute of other clothing than a thin pair of under-drawers, and their heads and faces are hidden in white cotton wraps, so that their neighbors may not, by recognizing them, have cause to wonder what crime they expiate. The leader staggers under the weight of a heavy cross about twenty feet high, and his companions, shivering with cold as the wind beats their naked bodies, carry thick bunches of the thorny cactus in their hands. The attendants place them in position, and at a given signal the procession moves, chanting a plaintive hymn to the time of the musician's pipe. At every second step the men strike themselves over the shoulders with the cactus, leaving a deeper scar with each blow, until the skin is broken and the lacerated flesh pours its blood in a carmine trail on the snow. Several are bound at the ankles by rawhide thongs, a dagger pointed at both ends being secured between the two feet in such a way that when they stumble, it stabs them in a most sensitive part. The sight becomes sickening with horror, and repressed moans of anguish fill the air as the cactus brushes afresh the streaming, quivering wounds. No one is allowed to retire, and when the cross-bearer sinks to the ground from exhaustion, the attendants quickly raise him and urge him on again with his heavy burden. The route is traced along the white road in crimson footsteps; and after parading the alleys of the town, the procession turns off toward a steep hill, in ascending which their bare feet are cut to the bone by the sharp projecting rocks. The eminence gained, preparations are made for a new and surpassing torture. The cross is laid upon the ground, and the bearer is so firmly bound to it by lengths of rawhide that the circulation of the blood is retarded, and a gradual discoloration of the body follows. His arms are outstretched along the transverse beam, to which a sword, pointed at both ends like the dagger before mentioned, is attached ; and if he allows them to drop a single inch from their original position, the weapon penetrates the flesh. Amid the unearthly groans of the bystanders and the shrill piping of the musician, the cross is raised, and the crucified turns his agonized face to heaven, while the blood slowly trickles from his wounds and a livid hue overspreads his skin. How long he remains is merely a question of endurance, for eventually he loses consciousness, and not until then is he released. At the conclusion of this barbarous performance, which occasionally results in death, the *penitentes* return to the Morada, and the celebration is brought to a close.

In personal appearance the New Mexicans are spare and brown-skinned. Their hair and eyes are lustrously black, and their speech is low and pleasant. You can not know how sweet the human voice is capable of being until you have heard one of their woman say," *No sabe*," or " *Quien sabe.*" She utters it with a gentle, melting, longing intonation, to be enjoyed and not to be described. But New Mexican women are not all sweetness and beauty. Their features are irregular, and their forms squat. Some of them study comfort more than delicacy, and in hot weather are content to flutter about in a chemise and flannel petticoat. Out of doors they swathe themselves in long black shawls, covering the head and part of the face in a picturesque manner that reminds one of the East. A friend of mine maintains that there is a still further similarity between the extremes of life here and those of ancient Palestine. The houses are primitive enough certainly, and the maidens carry earthen vessels of water on their heads in the same manner that Rebecca did in the time of the patriarchs.

The only American usually settled in the Mexican towns is the post trader, with a wife or a daughter, in whose house we perhaps find a piano, a sewing-machine, and a rocking-chair, things that strike us as being prodigious and exceptional luxuries. After a month of camp-life, indeed, the smallest suggestion of home and house comforts came upon us very gratefully. We had traveled days together without seeing a living soul, until we would have willingly exchanged a hundred miles of the mountains for a glance at a New England village. But bacon and bread had become appetizing, the shooting-coat had been altogether abandoned, and as the greenhorn, with the brim of his hat disreputably turned down, lay in his shelter tent, smoking in the evening after a hard day's march, he felt like a veteran.

CHAPTER IV.

AN UNBEATEN TRAIL.

The Luxuriant Vegetation of the Conejos Cañon.—Sleeping under Ice in June.—The Cañon of Los Piños.—The Head waters of the Rio Chama.—The Sublimity of Night in the Mountains.—Sam Abbey's Encounter with the Cinnamon Bear.—The Coyotes' Serenade.

FROM a camp near Guadalupe, which is one of the plazas of Conejos, we followed the main branch of the Conejos River for about three miles, and then diverged on a trail through a pass in the steep walls to the west, and over a heavily wooded acclivity, with a crest about eight hundred feet above the level. The way up the hill was obstructed in the earlier stages by fragments of rock scattered in every direction, like the *débris* of a spent shower of meteors ; and as we mounted higher, another difficulty appeared in a dense forest of cottonwood, with an almost impassable undergrowth of shrubs and brambles. The facility with which this tree adapts itself to circumstances is one of the marvels of the vegetable world. When it has room, it soars to a height of seventy feet, spreading itself out like an old yew ; but it seems to thrive equally well in a confined space, where hundreds of its species are limited in growth to six

4

fect, and concentrated within a few inches of each other. Its leaves are like those of the lilac, a small oval in shape, with the lightness and sensitiveness of the aspen and the glitter of the silver poplar. But most beautiful is the bark, which in nearly all the ages of the tree is a shade of soft gray, and as smooth on the surface as a piece of ivory.

Climbing higher, we became entangled in this maze of cottonwood, which hid us from one another, and knotted itself in our bridles and stirrups, making our progress more laborious than ever. The grass was tall and rank, and sprinkled with blue, yellow, red, and purple flowers, the blue and yellow vying with the sky and sun, which at intervals were revealed through a break in the thicket. Occasionally a breath of wind swept among the cottonwoods, and their leaves shook and glistened like the drops of a silvery rain.

So we went on, with our arms extended over our mules' heads to ward off the obstructing branches, until we came to a pile of moss-covered lava at the head of the farther slope. Beneath us was the junction of two branches of the main cañon —two deep cuttings, with high, precipitous banks, leading from an even ridge to a flat bottom. Here the cottonwoods were still more profuse and the other vegetation still more redundant. The bed of the cañon was matted by a luxuriant shrub, called, our Mexican guide told me, the jara, with leaves a vivid green and stalks a bright red. Underneath this there was a low rippling sound, and when we swept the branches aside, we discovered a brooklet running with the bluish water of freshly melted snows. Snows ? Yes : with all the abundance of foliage, in the middle of an exceptionally hot June, a white mantle still lay on the shady parts of this cañon, eight thousand feet above the level of the sea. The banks were covered with cottonwoods varying in height from six to seventy feet, all trembling, all gleaming, as the wind touched them. Some majestic pines, with rugged limbs and dusky green foliage, were superadded to these, and dense as the living timber was, thousands of dead trunks lay on the hillsides, where they had fallen in the last tempest. Ahead of us a cloud of blue smoke wreathed itself to heaven, and presently we came upon a wide patch of land wasted and blackened by fires that were still spreading.

As we went through the hollows the sound of our steps was drowned in the beds of mosses and ferns, and numberless wild flowers constantly tempted us to dismount and pick them.

Then, after resting a night, and on the next morning finding our tents sheathed in an armor of frozen rain, we struck into another labyrinth, crossing the main branch, and continuing on our way over fertile valleys and snowy ridges until we reached the head of a declivity looking down on the two arms of the cañon of Los Piños, which formed a junction.

If you would realize the scene, think of two awfully deep ravines, extending at an obtuse angle from each other, one toward the southwest, the other toward the east—two ravines with slanting walls of hemlock, fir, and pine which at their bases are only separated by the hair's breadth of a rushing stream, these walls forming themselves at intervals into perpendicular cliffs of green basaltic rock. Think of a tempestuous sky, with ragged storm-clouds careering in massive volumes overhead, and a perpetual twilight below casting weird shadows upon the lower slopes. Think of a strong wind whistling in fitful gusts around the corners of enormous bowlders held loosely in their places by a pebbly soil: of wintry gloom and tumultuous motion. Then, possibly, you will have an understanding of some of the elements that give the scene its impressive and peculiar grandeur.

For about four hours we meandered a trail not more than ten inches wide, worn in the left wall of the cañon stretching to the north. This precarious foothold was at least three hundred feet above the bed of the stream, which bubbled along like a vein of burnished metal, and at least four hundred feet below the upper edge of the wall. In some places it was overhung by crags or abutments of cavernous rock eroded into quaint resemblances of artificial things, and again it wound itself into the shadows of massive bowlders that seemed balanced on needle points. The timber was scarce here. A few charred pine stems, straight as arrows, shot into the air, divested of branch and leaf, intensely black in contrast with the pallid cottonwood trunks that lay in waste on the gravelly cañon-sides. Out on the point of a rock an eagle sat brooding, and swooped away in an ever-increasing circle when he saw us. The turbulent stream that foamed over the ledges in its course was silent at our height; but our voices were drowned in the steady roar of the wind, which swept through the cañon with the sound of the waters at Niagara. Overhead—what was there? A strip of brightest blue, dazzling in its purity; a constant drift of little puffs of white and great volumes of rainy gray that hurried on with wild messages into the distant east.

A frosted mass of snow lay here and there in the fissures, with threads of water trickling from it into the bed of the stream. Our breathing was labored, and our lungs felt raw and burning. The trail was graven across the brow of the rock in zigzags forming a succession of hills, in climbing which we were compelled to dismount and lead our mules. But a little farther on the cañon turned to the east, leaving in its curve an opening through the west wall by which we passed into a marshy basin surrounded by hills of pine and matted by a thick growth of shrubbery. Crossing this to its farther divide, we lost the trail, and the pack train was detained while several members of the party started off in different directions to look for it.

Just ahead of us, apparently separating two outlets of the valley, was a knoll, which I ascended in order to get a glimpse of the surrounding country. The wind had fallen by this time, and there was only a gentle soughing among the pines and firs. The path was strewn with logs, some so far decayed that they crumbled to dust under my feet, and others the fresh wreck of the last tempest. The air was balmy with the strong scent of resin, and ministered a grateful ease to my wearied lungs. Several brown squirrels, startled at my approach, darted into their hiding-places with a timid cry, and stared me out of countenance with their sparkling eyes. The least sound fell with distinctness in the hush, and awoke ghostly reverberations among the fastnesses of rock surrounding.

I climbed leisurely to the crest of the hill, and came suddenly to the very edge of a cliff looking down upon a scene that must have made a life-long impression on the most trivial mind. Seven or eight hundred feet below me was a chasm, extending twenty miles in a straight course, and imprisoned by precipitous heights heavily timbered with dusky trees. Far away into a dreamy space of blue these two chains of mountains rose and fell like the billows of a sea, with their ridges drawn against the sky as clearly as a silhouette, and their thick mantles of dark green, that seemed beds of soft mosses in the distance, spangled with rainbow crags of basalt and sandstone. The cliff on which I stood was a blood-red, and opposite to me were three sharp spires supported from the face of a yellow stone bluff, like the turret window of a Normandy house. But it was not the extent of the prospect nor the grandeur of form and color that made this scene so impressive. The sun was still high, and the sky without a fleck, yet the silent space below was steeped in a mellow, cloistral twilight. It was as though the earth had gone back in a dream to the time when men's feet were circumscribed by one garden. I was on the edge of a world where human heart had never beaten, and where human hand had never worked to take away the melancholy and sanctity of primitive nature. What influence was it that exerted itself upon me as I looked over those waves of hills, the dark ravine between, and the stilly forests enveloped in a profound haze? I felt a wild despair, a heaviness of heart, that I was glad enough to relieve in answering the call of the men with the pack train.

The trail had been found again, and turning to the right of the knoll, a few hundred feet farther on we entered a grove of noble pines with

brown-red bark, the shadows of which made a
blackness so deep and silent that we glanced
around warily as we passed under them. This
fear-inspiring quality was increased by the boom-
ing note of the screech-owl that anon broke out
among the topmost branches with the muffled
sound of a death-bell. The grass here was profuse again, and the wild flowers flashed out in
greater variety than ever. By-and-by we reached
the crest of a steep hill covered with cottonwoods, and descending this, we were underneath
the cliff on which I had stood half an hour before,
locked in a glen inclosed on three sides by pine-
covered walls; the fourth side abutted on the
ravine, with its vista of hills and mysteries of
blue. A little way below another cañon ran into
the main, and two noisy brooklets joined arms to
form the head waters of the Rio Chama.

Amid this solitude, so far away from home
and friends, we pitched our tents and lit our
camp fire. On one side of us there was a bank of
supple shrubs several feet high, with vagrant
daisies bestrewn in the moist earth around, and,
though no water could be seen, the voice of a
stream arose from under this bowery canopy in a
lightsome trill. The air was clear and exhilarat-
ing, and scented with the pungent balsam of the
pine and the languishing sweetness of the wild
rose. A sprightly humming-bird stole among the
flowers, and robbed them of their honey with his

dainty bill. But far prettier to me than this gaudy fellow, with his airs and graces, were the butterflies, especially those of a tiny species, bluish in color, looking like violets that had been torn from their stems by the wind, and by some fairy power endowed with wings. I think these beauties must grow by what they feed on, for hosts of them fluttered about the clusters of bluebells that are more plentiful in this piny mountain valley than on the heathery hills of Scotland.

And soon the night came—the night that in this region reveals as many wonders as it hides. The first indication of its approach was a glow on the sandstone bluffs, deepening every moment, until these masses of red and yellow seemed like jewels in the green surrounding them. The azure sky faded away into a sea of pearl, in which some stray patches of white were floating lazily. Beneath this tranquil space of exquisite color the pines in the cañon remained heavy and dark, wrapped in an unaltered gloom. But anon—marvelous touch! marvelous change!—the west was lighted by a sensuous crimson, growing warmer each moment and fast overspreading the whole heaven. The sky, the clouds, the bluffs, were suffused in the passionate light, and by degrees the dim ravine lying so coldly in the earth was struck by the ruddy glow that kissed the embattled forests on the slopes, until the red pines blushed like maples in the autumn. For a sublime moment all the earth and heaven was swept by the flame, and the white tents in the glen confessed it in a shade of pink. Then it expired by as many changes as it came, and the sky became wan and cold. The shadows spread out their arms farther and farther, and the ravine became fathomless in a mysterious darkness that, impenetrable as it was, seemed to admit the vision into its depths.

The blaze of the camp fire leaped high, and the pine logs crackled merrily in the frosty air. By-and-by the stars came out, and the mountain ridges were illuminated by a phosphorescent light like that of St. Elmo, which men at sea sometimes see burning on the yard-arms, and believe to be the spirits of their dead comrades.

From this memorable camp we struck down the cañon, and again pitched our tents where the west fork of the Chama enters the east between two high embankments of rocky soil. We lay here for several days, and here we had our first taste of sport. The country was full of game, and a trained hunter need not have gone far in any direction to obtain an interview with either black, cinnamon, or grizzly bear. A Mexican who joined us at the town of Conejos borrowed ten cartridges and my carbine from me. He returned eight of the cartridges, and brought into camp a grouse and a magnificent deer. But a military exploring party finds no time for sporting—at least, ours did not find any; and unless the game came into camp, or ran against us on the road, we seldom had a chance to spend our powder.

One afternoon, however, Sam Abbey, one of the packers, ran into camp, with a pale face and his revolver drawn. "I—saw—a—bear—within—six—feet—of—me—and—it—laughed—at—me!" he exclaimed breathlessly. "Come—along—boys—an'—let's—have—a—shot!"

He had been lying asleep on the grass a short distance away when a panting sound awoke him, and as he opened his drowsy eyes he saw an enormous cinnamon bear gazing at him and smacking its rough lips. No wonder he was scared. A cinnamon bear is a terrible antagonist for a man with only a revolver to defend himself; and as Sam raised himself on his elbows, the ruthless monster studied him, with the intention of selecting a soft part to begin with evident in its small, ferocious, hungry-looking eyes. Our valiant comrade sighed, and sorrowfully cocked his six-shooter, for he knew that if he fired and missed a vital part, the subsequent proceedings would have no pleasurable interest for him. But the bear pricked its ears at the click of the hammer, and, with a laudable desire to avoid difficulties, waddled away down the hollow of the river. Sam could now feel the earth under him again, and sped to camp with the news of his adventure.

Mr. Karl, our assistant topographer, responded

to his call for volunteers, and went to the scene of the encounter with the hero, who now averred that the bear did not laugh, but "kinder grinned."

Poor Bruin had crossed the river, and was quietly ascending the opposite bank, when his pursuers espied him and pointed their carbines at him. Apparently understanding their intentions, he turned round and ran down the bank to have fair fight with them; but before he reached the bottom three bullets plowed through his body, and he rolled against a bowlder—a dead bear. May he rest in peace! Better eating we never had in our mess. His meat was stewed, roasted, and fried. It was palatable in every form, tender as a spring lamb's hind-quarter, juicy as the standing ribs of a prime Herefordshire ox, and of as agreeable a flavor as venison.

The night following this episode was starlight and frosty, and our little company, reduced in number to six by the absence of Lieutenant Morrison, Mr. Clark, and two others, gathered around a sparkling fire of logs. The mountain ridges were pale with nebulous light, like the gleaming white of the aurora borealis. The ravine was profoundly dark and silent, and our voices sounded with singular clearness in the crisp air. We were instinctively drawn nearer to our companions by the knowledge of our loneliness, like castaways on an ocean, and the men who had been utter strangers to each other six weeks before were united as closely as brothers. Suddenly a wild, despairing, horrible clamor broke the silence of the cañon, and was repeated thrice in muffled echoes from the sandstone cliffs. Our conversation abruptly ceased, and we—or those of us to whom this far western life was new—listened in dreadful suspense. The mules rushed past us, with dilating eyes and ears erect. A second time the cry, loud and demoniac as the glee of an escaped madman, awoke the ringing echoes. "Coyotes," some one suggested, and it was these mongrel wolves that made this dismal chorus in their revels over the carcass of the dead bear. Many a night afterward they stole about the outskirts of our camp, and disturbed us with their devil-like howling. Alone they do not often venture to attack a man, but in large numbers, and especially when led by a white wolf, they are dangerous company. Their bark is curiously deceptive, and sometimes when we were startled by an outcry that seemed to come from a pack of wolves, we looked back to see two or three mean little coyotes trotting away, with a hang-dog confession of cowardice in their bushy tails.

The coyote has been amusingly described by Dr. Eliot Coues, who in occupying himself as a naturalist deprives America of a genuine humorist.

"The barking wolf or coyote," Dr. Coues says, "is by far the most abundant carnivorous animal in almost every part of the West. Practically it is a nuisance; theoretically it compels a certain degree of admiration by its irrepressible positivity of character and its versatile nature. If its genius has nothing essentially noble or lofty about it, few animals possess so many and so various attributes, or act them out with such dogged perseverance. Ever on the alert, and keenly alive to a sense of danger, it yet exhibits the coolest effrontery when its path crosses ours. The main object of its life seems to be the satisfying of a hunger which is always craving, and to this aim all its cunning, impudence, and audacity are mainly directed.

"Much has been written concerning the polyglot serenades of the coyote, by those who have been unwilling listeners, but it is difficult to convey an adequate idea in words of the noisy confusion. One must have spent an hour or two vainly trying to sleep before he is in condition to appreciate the full force of the annoyance. It is a singular fact that the howling of two or three gives an impression that a score are engaged, so many, so long drawn are the notes, and so uninterruptedly are they continued by one individual after another. A short sharp bark is sounded, followed by several more in quick succession, the time growing faster and the pitch higher, till they run together into a long-drawn lugubrious howl, in the highest possible key. The same strain is taken up again and again by different members of the pack, while from a greater distance, the deep melancholy baying of the more wary ones breaks in to add to the discord, till the very leaves of the trees seem quivering to the inharmonious sounds. It is not true, as asserted by some, that the coyotes howl only just after dark and at daylight. Though they may be noisiest at these times, when the pack is gathering for a night's foraging, or dispersing again to their dismal retreats, I know that they give tongue at any time during the night. They are rarely if ever heard in daytime, though frequently to be seen, at least in secluded regions. Ordinarily, however, they spend the day in quiet, out-of-the-way places, among rocks, in thick copses, etc., and seek their prey mainly by night, collecting for this purpose into packs as already noticed.

"The coyote, although a carnivore, is a very indiscriminate feeder, and nothing seems to come amiss which is capable of being chewed and swallowed. From the nature of the region it inhabits, it is often hard-pressed for food, particularly in the winter season. Besides such live game as it can surprise and kill, or overpower by persevering pursuit and force of numbers, it feeds greedily on all sorts of dead animal matter. To procure this, it resorts in great numbers to the vicinity of settlements, where offal is sure to be found, and surrounds the hunter's camp at night. It is well known to follow for days in the trail of a traveling party, and each morning just after camp is broken it rushes in to claim whatever eatable refuse may have been left behind. But it can not always find a sufficiency of animal food, and is thus made frugivorous and herbivorous. Particularly in the fall it feeds extensively upon the juicy, soft scarlet fruit of various species of prickly pear, and in the winter upon berries of various sorts, particularly those of the juniper and others.

"Coyotes are so very annoying that a variety of means are used to destroy them. They may be shot, of course, but to hunt them in the daytime is uncertain, and hardly worth the trouble, while night shooting is still more laborious and unsatisfactory. Their cunning, inquiring disposition is ordinarily more than a match for man's ingenuity in the way of traps. The most certain, as well as the easiest method of obtaining them is by poisoning the carcass of a dead animal or butcher's offal with strychnine. There is no doubt also that the odor of asafœtida is attractive to them, and a little of this drug rubbed into the poisoned meat greatly heightens the chances of their eating it. Since after eating the poison they suffer greatly from thirst, it is well to place a tub of water conveniently at hand, which generally keeps them from making off for water, and so being lost."

CHAPTER V.

MOUNTAINEERING IN THE SAN JUAN RANGE.

A Difficult March—The Startling Features of a Mountain Marsh—Our Topographer's Deer—A Camp in Utter Solitude—Adventure as a Monomania—The Snow Flowers of an Alpine Lake—On the Top of Banded Peak—Two Hundred Miles at a Glance—Mr. Clark's Peril—Head First Down a Cañon.

FROM the station at the forks of the river an excursion was made to some of the highest peaks in the San Juan range. Our route lay up the western branch of the cañon, between the high embankments before alluded to, which were so regular that they seemed the work of artifice rather than of nature, and resembled the deep cuttings of an English railway more than anything else. A narrow bed of shining pebbles and sand, with a noisy stream foaming in the center, divided them for the distance of a mile, beyond which they expanded into a beautiful valley, with a shady border of swarming fir and pine, and overhanging cliffs of carmine sandstone.

Farther on they almost interlocked each other again, and became so steep that our animals could no longer find a secure foothold on them, in consequence of which we were compelled to make a circuit of several miles through a closely packed forest and by the borders of a marsh before we again reached a clearing. In places the mountain torrents had washed a rough channel nine feet deep in the earth, and great lifeless trees, with their long-armed roots dissevered, were piled in confusion across our path.

Something opposed us at every step. At one moment we were netted in a thick growth of shrubs, the elastic branches of which switched our faces like a birch rod, and the next moment our nerves were disturbed by the unpleasant sensation of the mules sinking from under us in a bog. There is no telling a Western marsh. The ground before you appears as firm as rock itself, and there is nothing to indicate or excite the least suspicion of its treacherous character. Your mule quakes and snorts, and before you are well aware of what has happened, he has, with good luck, dragged himself through the mire, and stands, quivering in every muscle, on solid ground again.

But these were minor difficulties, and if there be a mountaineer among my readers, he will think such commonplace matters too trivial for notice. In truth, the real hard work of the day had not begun, although noon found us toiling toward the end of our eighth mile. The sierras ahead of us, viewed from the high ground in the rear of our camp, looked scarcely more than a mile or two distant, so delusively clear was the atmosphere, and now they seemed to be as far away as ever— far away, yet near ; so near that it seemed possible for an outstretched arm to reach them. Their heights of stratified rock overshadowed the shady green foothills and the red-lipped cliffs. The floods of sunshine pouring down upon them softened their asperities and warmed the beautiful mauve color and lustrous snowfields of the peaks.

Anon we came to a halt for the purpose of deliberating on our farther progress. The right bank suddenly twisted itself inward, and compressed the cañon to half its former width. On one side we were obstructed by a bluff, almost precipitous, and completely netted by a most prolific growth of cottonwoods; on the other side by a great sandstone cliff, eight or nine hundred feet high, with a projecting shelf overhanging the river that rushed through these narrows with overwhelming impetuosity. It was impossible to drive the pack animals through the cottonwoods, and though a mule is capable of any ordinary feat of agility, it is not equal to the task of walking the sheer walls of a cliff. The current of the river was deep and strong, the bottom a pitfall of slippery rocks, and wherever a little soil had drifted, a swarm of small trees crowded off every other thing.

But the river was our only way out of the net, and, trusting to luck, we splashed into the giddy rapids. At one moment our animals plunged up to the shoulders in the fierce tumult of waters; the next moment they staggered as if about to fall, with their hoofs caught between two ledges of rock; the next they were secure on a shoal; and so, with alternations of excitement and confidence, we reached a low embankment, steep, and thick with cottonwoods, but passable for a short distance. The cliff at the gateway of the upper cañon receded from the river, and, acquiring greater height, ended in a line of lucid peaks, which effectually inclosed the cañon on one side with a wall about two thousand feet high, unbroken, except at the foot, where there was a wave of low hills. About four miles above, another range extended from this, and guarded the river with a varied and beautiful series of pinnacles and domes, barren, and hoary with snow also; and to the left of these again, on the right bank of the river, several yet higher and more graceful peaks rose with clearly defined outlines against the sky that they seemed to pierce.

Lieutenant Morrison, Mr. Clark, and the writer went on in advance of the packers, and a sudden turn in the bush showed us, not more than twenty yards away, a beautiful deer, which was browsing with its broadside toward us. "It's my birthday; I'm always in luck on my birthday," whispered Clark as he quickly dismounted, unstrapped his carbine from his saddle, and took a long steady aim. For three weeks our mess had been without fresh meat, excepting the bear's, and we already seemed to smell the savory steam of venison cutlets. Clark fired, and a second later the deer bounded into the thicket uninjured. He intently regarded the breech of his gun. "It's out of order ; I must have it fixed," he said with delicious equanimity, as he remounted his animal ; and we were charitable enough to believe that something was the matter with it.

Starting in the morning from an elevation of about 8,000 feet, where the air was warm even to sultriness, we had muffled ourselves in three suits of winter underclothing, and a keen wind sweeping through the gulches proved the wisdom of our precaution early in the afternoon. Not only was the air cold ; the sentiment and color of the scene were bleak also. Here, in contrast with the deep coloring of the cliffs, the heavy gloom and massive foliage of the undulating hills at the head waters of the east branch, the mountains were bare, and as pinnacled as icebergs, and as polished as the track of a glacier. The snow lay in rings on their summits like a fringe of ermine, and down the face of a kingly cliff, apparently sheltered from the sun in a deep fissure, was a ribbon of the same fleecy white. The hue of the rocks alternated between gray and a delicate shade of mauve, darkening in the recesses to purple. Overhead the sky was a perfect blue. The opposite wall of the cañon rose from high cottonwood bluffs, extending into high table-lands, and serrated by another battlement of snowy peaks. The form of every object was marvelously distinct in the rarefied air, and stood out from the rest in clear relief, with the chilly sentiment of a marble statue about it ; and our eyes searched in vain for a bit of warm color or a manifestation of nature's softer mien.

We picked our way on either side of the stream as opportunity offered, crossing from the right to the left by turns, climbing and descending cliffs by thread-like paths, cutting a passage through tangles of cottonwood, now trusting to the bed of the river or following its rim of loose rocks, and then running in a semicircle over the table-lands to avoid some insuperable obstacle in the ravine below. We had been on the march ten hours, and the sun bent nearer the obdurate peaks of gray as if to salute them ; the ridges burned scarlet, and the snowfields and all things were swept by a rosy glow. But the glory was evanescent, and, passing away, it left the cañon colder and whiter than ever. We made camp on a bit of level ground near the turning of the stream to the south, with barricades of rock on four sides, and innumerable peaks drawn in a zigzag line on the sky. Not the faintest sound broke the utter solitude—neither the flap of a wing, the cry of beast, the rustle of the cottonwood, nor the clamor of the swollen river. A mighty waterfall pouring for a thousand feet down the vertical front of a cliff in a continuous line of white, so smooth in its motion that it was scarcely distinguished from snow, and a rougher torrent leaping over a high ledge into a chasm, were alone heard in a low ringing sound, like the dying vibrations of a bell. All else was silent and motionless; and as the sky was transmuted to a dark blue, as the stars, gaining luster with the advancing night, shone on the frigid peaks and edged them with light, as the gloom and iciness worked upon us with depressing influence, we better understood the melancholy that Mr. Ruskin attributes to all mountain scenery.

Among the members of the expedition was a young man from one of the Middle States, a fresh graduate of Georgetown College, who was destined for the profession of law. He was bright, generous, and amiable; but his great ambition was to write thrilling letters, depicting the perils of our life, to his friends at home, and he rode along from day to day plotting horrors that might by some disastrous mischance befall us. When our rations were reduced to dry bread and coffee, he smiled with diabolic complacency—a willing sacrifice himself, on account of the compensation he derived from the materials our sufferings afforded him. He was not satisfied with swallowing mud for water; he had a secret wish that we might all be prostrated by thirst, and opportunely rescued a few seconds before the minute when help would be too late. He pined and lost his appetite if there were no rattlesnakes near camp, and he was overjoyed when one morning he found a deadly centipede in his bed. I believe a chasm was never safely passed that a pang did not enter his heart—not that he would have rejoiced over a brother's broken neck, for he was a sensitive and sympathetic fellow in most concerns, but he was as sorry when we escaped a catastrophe as he would have been had we suffered it. His mania was for abundant discomforts and "hair's-breadth 'scapes," such as are nowhere so common as in the daily newspapers; and I have no doubt that he framed, if he did not write, the words of many an imaginary dispatch to the Associated Press describing how the whole expedition tumbled over a precipice, and bounced from rock to rock for a distance of several thousand feet, "narrowly escaping fatal injuries."

He did not accompany us on this side trip to the San Juan range, or he might have curdled the blood—a mysterious process discovered by some astute story writer since the time of Mr. Harvey—of his little audience at home. Our limbs were all sound in the end, but we had a surprising number of little accidents and inconveniences, which must have excited his imagination to the point at which authorship of a dime novel is possible.

After a sound sleep in the frosty open air, we started early next morning through a gorge some distance to the left of the greater cataract, reaching from the level to the summit of the cliff under the shelter of which we had rested during the night. The lower part was at an angle of repose, and was roughly paved with detritus, but the upper part was a mere crevice in the cliff, revealing the bare sides of the mountain. We succeeded very well, however, until we were within a few hundred feet of the top, when we encountered a vast quantity of ice and snow, which compelled us to unload the mules and carry the packs by hand —a task which occupied us four hours. The first bench reached, we found a wild-looking valley undulating before us, with a dense undergrowth, and wide marshes wavy with tall blades of emerald grass swaying in the wind. A little farther on we saw ourselves reflected on the clear surface of a blue lake, separated from another circle of crystal water by a narrow isthmus, and dotted on its borders by a variety of wild flowers, which spread their gay ranks forward until they were tipped by the ripples, and backward until their pliant little stems were seen sprouting out of the snow, as if that crusted mass of icy white yielded them their miracles of lovely color. One pretty little thing we christened the nun-flower, because of its sweet, modest colors—a ring of rich brown near the stamen, and lavender fading into white near the edge.

Farther on still, we regained solid footing on some cropping rock extending to the base of another cliff, about four hundred feet above us, the ascent of which was made by a trail over loose rocks tramped into shape by game—a narrow, dangerous trail, but the only one that we could follow. And here again a large bed of snow stood in our way, varying in depth from a few inches to twenty feet, with a brittle surface of ice, over which the mules labored painfully. The summit was rounded into another basin, set with several more lakes, bordered by light green marsh grass, and so smooth and wonderfully clear that the rock-ribs of the valley and the sky and mountain-tops seemed repeated in their depths. Snow lay everywhere, prismatic in the sunshine, and melting as the day warmed into hundreds of tiny rivulets. But we were still between high walls, with a few sharp pinnacles above us, and no extended view of the surrounding country. We climbed a hill on which not a grain of sand or soil could be seen, and from the top of this we went along a saddle of rock to camp under the protection of a rising peak. But we had scarcely unpacked the mules when the wind changed, and beat against us with pitiless violence during the rest of the night. And thus ended our second day of mountaineering in the San Juan range. We had made four miles in eleven hours of continuously laborious travel, which fact is the best criterion of the difficulties of the route.

On the next day we attained by some perilous climbing a truncated cone of rock, about thirty feet in diameter, without a bit of moss, a blade of grass, or a shrub on its plainly marked stratification. And this was the summit of Banded Peak, 13,500 feet above the level of the sea, rising among a multitude of other peaks so close together and numerous that Lieutenant Morrison well compared them to the pipes of a great organ. In the far south was Mount Taylor, 158 miles away, in New Mexico; in the west, the Chasca range, on the borders of Arizona; in the north and east, Sierra Blanca, Baldy, and the Sangré del Cristo, near Fort Garland; in every direction clusters of pointed rock, row after row of peaks, thrust defiantly above the clouds to the heavens. In the same magnificent reach we could trace the Navajo, the Chama, and the Los Piños, gathering their head waters from the lakes in the basins around Banded Peak, and winding all a-glitter through the blue and white mazes of ravines and cataracts. The wind blustered about us as though it would drive us over the ledge, and several ptarmigan tamely approached us, and hopped aside in utter bewilderment when we threw some stones at them, so unused were they to the sight of man.

The nearer objects in the sublime outlook appeared to be so very near, and the farther objects so very far, that we could easily imagine that it was not an area of 200 miles we gazed down upon, but the world itself. And a cheerless, tumultuous, grief-stricken world it seemed to be— the sky a frosty blue, the adjacent rocks purple in the shadow, gray or mauve in the light, and the lowlands confused blots of brown and heavy green. Even these colors were subdued in the distance to a dull yellow spread over the swelling plains, from which the precipices were exalted as out of a shipless sea.

But this was in the flood light of the afternoon, and as the brisk wind swept up some clouds in the west, the whole scene was changed. The mountains were wrapped in the folds of a mist of the purest white, and their outlines loomed upon us in vapory phantoms. The clouds were rent into columns of gray, and instead of looking down on to the chaotic upheaval of a continent, it was as though we were on the verge of a fairyland. And when the sun burst through the storm, the rocks streamed with moisture, which, reflecting the brazen light, gave them the appearance of having a glittering armor of burnished silver, and a gorgeous rainbow spread its triumphal arch across the sky, while all the lowlands were vague and moist under the masses of cloud that drifted far below us.

After taking a series of observations with the gradientor, aneroid, and barometer, we made a record of our visit, and placed it in a tin tube under a cairn or monument, for the information of future explorers—a custom invariably adopted by the Wheeler expedition. The two packers and the animals had been left at the camp of the previous day, and we now prepared to rejoin them by what appeared to be a shorter path than that by which we ascended. We climbed down a perilous cliff on to a narrow terrace of rock, and then, to our dismay, we found that we had overlooked a field of ice and snow lying at as acute an angle as possible on the face of the mountain for a distance of several hundred feet.

We tried to retrace our way and regain the summit, but we could not scale the cliff without endangering our lives, and the only feasible plan that suggested itself was to cut a series of steps in the snow. We stood cogitating at the brink of the blinding white sheet, undecided as to which course to take, when Mr. Clark incautiously stamped his heels on the edge to try its brittleness. His foot slipped from under him, and the next moment we were thrilled by seeing him sliding down the mountain with the velocity of a flash of light. He was in a sitting posture, his hair was blown back, and his hat slowly rolled down after him. At the bottom of the slope was a narrow gutter, leading up from which was another snow-bank. If the impetus of the descent had been great enough to force him up this, he would have been shot into a deep chasm. But he carried a spiked tripod, which made an excellent alpenstock, and with fine presence of mind he plunged this into the snow between his legs, slid half way up it, and suddenly came to a stop. He felt himself with his hands, in a dazed manner, as though he was under the impression that he had left something behind — which he had done; the same thing, in fact, that hushes Tatters's voice when the Shaughraun announces in the play that the Fenian's refuge is discovered; in short, "the sate of a man's breeches."

The rest of the way was passed in safety, and the following day we joined the main camp at the forks of the Chama.

I ventured to return ahead of my companions, and soon lost the trail. About two o'clock in the afternoon I stood on the river-bottom, with a shoal of quicksand before me, and two very steep and high embankments on either hand. I had to avoid the quicksands of course; but the embankments were nearly perpendicular and covered with a thick grass that had already worn the sides of my boots to the smoothness of glass. I could not stand, so slippery was the surface, much less lead my animal; and after many vain endeavors I decided to mount her. I succeeded after a great deal of stumbling in getting half way up the embankment, when, alas ! the lateral strain broke the saddle-girth, and I rolled like a log toward the bottom of the cañon. Down I went fifty feet or more, my cartridges, eyeglasses, and a haunch of venison following, until I was caught in the midriff by a providential bowlder. I looked up the slope for the mule, and she patiently stood where I had so unexpectedly left her, looking down upon me with a mutely sympathetic glance. Luckily I was not seriously hurt ; and after taking my boots off, reached the top without further difficulty.

CHAPTER VI.

ISSUE DAY AT AN INDIAN AGENCY.

The Trader's Store at Tierra Amarilla—A Gathering of Utes, Navajos, and Apaches—The Subordination of Women— The Beauty of the Young Squaws—How Arrows are Poisoned—The Tribulations of an Indian Agent.

TEN miles south of the Forks of the Chama, across the New Mexican boundary line, we traveled over a low-lying plateau, realizing in all its features the cultivated and orderly magnificence of an English park, with the difference that for oaks there were pines—pines that matched the oaks in size, age, strength, and stateliness ; not packed together densely, but towering to a height of eighty or a hundred feet at even intervals, with a clear space wide enough to allow a carriage to pass between them. Nor was the regularity with which these superb trees were set the only point of their resemblance to the woodlands of the old country. The ground was perfectly level except where a little knoll broke its monotony, and covered with a short, thick, smooth carpet of grass, that only needed a little care, a little rolling and clipping, to make it as lustrous and elastic as the baronial lawns of England. In places an opening occurred, in which, as if to complete the picture of pastoral order and culture, great flocks of sheep were grazing, attended by dirtily picturesque half-breeds and Mexicans.

A few miles beyond we reached Tierra Amarilla, another Mexican town duplicating all the features of Conejos, and here we pitched our tents for several days. We had not received a mail for some weeks, nor spoken to a soul outside our own party ; and though Tierra Amarilla is suicidally vacuous as a residence, it was to us a potential Paris in the wilderness. The porch outside the trader's store was crowded with Mexicans, chattering Spanish and smoking cigaritas. A few Indians crouched inside, looking at us and criticising our dress. While the trader was selecting our letters, I noticed a very big straw hat on the counter with a very small pair of legs sitting under it. The legs dangled against the boards, and presently

I was aware of a boy's voice under the hat which directed itself to me.

"Do you belong to the Wheeler expedition?"

"Yes."

"And have you been in the mountains?"

"Yes."

"I guess you come from the East too?"

"Yes."

"Ah," continued the treble voice pathetically, "you must find life very different out here from what it is there. *I* do. I came from Indianapolis. It's a big place that. And, I say, wouldn't you like to see a nice frame house and some big trees, and to have some peaches? Ah," he went on, without waiting for an answer, "*I* would. And some white boys to play with. There ain't any white boys here; they are all *greasers*, and we don't call them white because they are brown. They swear and chew, and don't know how to play soldiers. Oh, it's very different here from what it is in Indianapolis!"

He was silent for a moment as he dreamed of the charms of Indianapolis, and in the mean time one of the Indians arose from his squatting position on the floor and shuffled out with a blanket wrapped around his loins. "He doesn't look like Osceola or King Philip, does he?" the small boy resumed in a contemptuous tone; and then he added: "You'll see plenty of Indians on Saturday; that's issue day, and I'm the Indian agent's son."

The agency was a long one-storied adobe house, whitewashed, with a wide portico running around it, and built in a hollow square. On Saturday the small boy came to camp for us, and provided us with chairs in the courtyard. Two butchers were cutting up five enormous beeves, and a storeroom was filled from the floor to the ceiling with sacks of flour, kegs of gunpowder, and bags of shot. The day was dazzling, and soon after nine o'clock the beneficiaries of the occasion came from the neighboring encampment in a constant stream. They had donned the garb of festivity, and were weighted with rainbow-colored blankets, feathers, bead-work, and flashing silver ornaments. All were mounted on ponies, and all carried great leafy branches of trees to protect their heads from the sun. In some instances a whole family was mounted on one horse, the chief in the saddle, with a little boy in front of him, and the squaw behind, with a papoose strapped to her back. In other instances each member of the family had a separate animal, and the chief led, with his wife and children following in a string. Every face was painted with vermilion on the cheek, on the forehead, or around the lids of the eye, the last producing a most diabolical effect.

The young squaws wore shawls of red and other bright colors, necklaces of beads, heavy earrings, and belts of silver lozenges. But those who were no longer pretty fell behind in rags and misery. The chiefs were wrapped up in blankets, although the day was very hot, and many of them wore felt hats of obsolete pattern. They were armed with shot-guns, revolvers of old-fashioned make, bows and steel-headed arrows.

The method of poisoning the arrows, as it was explained to us at the agency, is peculiar. The Indians take the robe of a freshly killed buffalo, antelope, or deer, with a coat of fat clinging to it; and having previously gathered several rattlesnakes, they goad the reptiles with a sharpened stick to strike at it. An arrow head dipped first in water and then in the robe stung by the snakes is poisonous even when the fat is completely dry and months old. The liver of animals is used in the same manner, and according to frontiersmen, the moment it is struck by the snake it changes from its natural color to a bright green.

The Indians came into the courtyard more numerously than ever. There were Utes, Apaches, and Navajos. The Utes and Apaches can scarcely be distinguished from one another. They are both marked by aquiline noses, small eyes, a dull copper complexion, and a treacherous expression. The Navajos, on the contrary, have a rich brown complexion, large beautiful eyes, very broad shoulders, and a frank, happy, intelligent look that is very winsome. Their dress is a short tunic of some fancy cotton print and breeches of the same material, with black socks and buckskin moccasins. While the agency was properly that of the Utes and Apaches, the Navajos also had claims for rations. When the tribes had halted their horses in the corral, the women came and sat under the portico, while the men sauntered through the yard smoking vile tobacco in corn-cobs. An apparently better-natured assemblage could not easily be found, and one thing especially noticeable was the tender care of the mothers for their chubby, big-headed, naked babies. But as soon as the issue began the greed and dishonesty of the people were brought into stronger light than their good nature had been before.

"They try every imaginable trick to get a double allowance," said the Indian agent to me as he marshaled the squaws in line, "and they occasionally succeed."

When the women had been put in order, he passed down the line and gave to each of them a small ticket entitling her to ten pounds of beef for every member of her family. Then he passed down the line again and gave to each another ticket, entitling her to ten pounds of flour; but the moment he had finished his rounds, he was besieged by a frantic crowd vowing that they had not received tickets, although they had just come out of the line. The chiefs came to the support of their squaws, and increased the clamor. Some of the women actually had tickets in their hands while they were flatly protesting that they had received none; and seven small children who had been seated with their mothers five minutes before, were brought forward as the orphans of the tribe, with a demand for special rations. The agent was browbeaten and confused, until he refused to issue a single ticket more ; and the women finding their entreaties unavailing, then rushed off to the storehouse to obtain their food in exchange for their orders. The beef was passed to them through a small window about four feet from the ground, in enormous joints, so heavy that occasionally a poor squaw could not tackle her share, and, when she attempted to carry it off, let it fall, to the vast amusement of the chiefs. The men never offered the least assistance, and the women struggled across the courtyard with their heavy loads and packed them upon the horses.

After the flour and beef had been distributed, small quantities of tea and coffee were given to the old men and women, and the chiefs were supplied with powder and shot. There were many ludicrous scenes, and many little quarrels. No one was satisfied, although every one had been treated with the greatest fairness. By noon most of them had received their supplies and gone home to their wigwams. A few remained to haggle with the agent, and others loafed outside the courtyard, or, seated in the middle of the street, gambled their rations away with the Mexicans.

As we started to go to camp, the small boy, who had been absent for some time, came running after us. "Good-by," he said. "I have been having a splendid time; two Americans have just come from Denver, and we have been playing soldiers ever since I left you. It's high !" he added, in the vernacular of Indianapolis, as he hastened back to the martial amateurs.

The next day was the Fourth of July, and when we awoke in camp, each man fired a shot from his revolver, and one flew a patriotic pocket handkerchief from his tent.

CHAPTER VII.

THE MIRACULOUS MESA COUNTRY.

A Prospect of Suffering—A Counterpart of the Yellowstone—The Cities Wrought by Rain—On the Summit of the Continental Divide—The Rock Fantasies of the Cañon Blanco—A Region without Water and without Vegetation—The Extinct Races of New Mexico and their Ruins—The Wonders of Pueblo Pintado.

WE left Tierra Amarilla to enter a section of Arizona and the northwest corner of New Mexico, reputed to be so wild, desolate, and unknown that our undertaking was threatened with the chance of many privations and no little peril. We were advised to fill our canteens and trust in Providence at the start, and were told that we would not find any running streams in a distance of ninety miles; that the only water would be found in springs far apart, and pools formed by rain. The prospect was not encouraging. Parts of the territory had never been explored before, and the remainder was known only to a few cattle-herders and Indians. It was a treacherous country moreover, with many quicksands and marshes, in which the horses might suddenly sink too deep to be recovered. A skirmish with marauding Utes in the Washington Pass was also counted among the possibilities, and our food supplies were limited to twenty-one days, the shortest time in which the journey could be made.

With little in our favor and much against us, we started out. Soon after leaving the town we entered the desert—a region of high tablelands, *mesas* in the Spanish, from 7,000 to 10,000 feet above the level of the sea, by which the country for miles is divided into deep channels, like the dry courses of a stream winding among innumerable islands. These mesas are not like mountains except in height. They rise 400 or 500 feet from the plain by a precipitous slope of rock and sand, fostering forests of dwarf pine and fir, above which is a distinct belt of sandstone strata reaching to the summit. But their summits, instead of having the craggy formation of a mountain, roll off into table-lands, heavily timbered and occasionally marshy. As we stand in one of the cañons that divide them, some of them resemble great iron-clads, with projecting rams at the bows, and are oblong in shape; others are in the form of rotundas, the same height from the plain all around; and others again rise from the level by an easy slope, ending in a superb bluff several hundred feet high. They are one of the most curious features of Western scenery, and are more impressive than many higher forms. The sandstone strata is miraculously varied in color. Sometimes it is a decided yellow, with a vein of blood-red running through it; sometimes a metallic dark green, like bronze; and sometimes a faint shade of blue. Both strong chemical hues and mild intermediate tints abound, and are equally bewildering in their intensity and delicacy. The constitution of the mesas is not less remarkable than their color. Usually they comprise the ordinary successive layers of rock, but in some instances the walls are built as by hand, of small rectangular blocks laid as methodically as the bricks of a house. A commoner formation consists of large square slabs, two or three inches in thickness, and thin, slate-like sheets, rough on the edge.

About ten miles from Tierra Amarilla we crossed a portion of the level paved with square blocks of water-deposit sandstone, as evenly and apparently with as much design as Broadway is paved; and out of the crevices between these blocks, growing from them, to all appearances, was a thick battalion of pines. At another point we saw a mesa with a slanting abutment, at least 400 feet high, erected with the same precision and in the same manner. A photograph or wood-engraving can not give any idea of the wonders of the mesas, the peculiarity of which is in their profuse color. The surrounding land is an untilled solitude, with scarce a single attractive feature. The soil is either white or yellow, and affords slender support to a multitude of sage-bushes with bodies gnarled and knotted like the children of infirmity, the leaden hue of which spreads itself over the plain until it seems to be a slowly rising mist. Where the mesas are, the pines on the slopes are blots of sombre greenness, enlivened by the chromatic belt of sandstone, and a crown of fresher vegetation above. The white earth, the grayish green of the shrubs, the strangely variegated and ponderous rocks, together reveal a new phase of nature, for the like of which I can only refer the reader to his own imagination. Underneath the sage-bushes the purple flower of the wild verbena grows—how, in the parched soil that seems too sterile for the commonest weeds, is a mystery—and the savage cactus, bristling with vindictive thorns, blossoms in a flower as tender-looking as a rose-bud. The mesas are the work of water acting on friable rock and clay, and their history is to be read in every ditch. The composition of the earth is such that after a storm it is mapped with vertical fissures ready to yield to the next fall of rain, and constantly enlarging into wide channels, which will anon encircle and work out a whole tract of land. The smallest drain has stratified walls, sheer from the level to the stream, and in some places we found a circular basin, dry, yet more verdant than the surrounding country, inclosed by the same kind of perpendicular walls, varying from three to five feet in height.

Our first day's march from Tierra Amarilla was short and comfortable, and we camped for the night on the Chama, obtaining some speckled trout for supper. But on the second day we traveled twenty-five miles in order to reach a muddy little creek, with water of the color and thickness, but without the flavor, of a rich cream. On the third day we made nearly twenty-nine miles in a heavy storm, through a section equaling, and probably surpassing, the famous Yellowstone region in its natural wonders. As in the latter valley, the principal rocks are of mutable sandstone, wrought by wind, dust, and rain into forms of inconceivable beauty. There is less of the grotesque than in the wonder-land of Montana, or in Colorado's Garden of the Gods, however; for Nature has here wrought the phenomenal without running riot.

From our camp we ascended a hill belonging to a ridge that partly incloses a small valley, walled in on the opposite side by white cliffs, ornamented with scroll-work as by the chisel of a sculptor. The ridge undulates by an easy grade toward the middle, where it descends into a wide gap, opening a vista of mountains beyond; and in the center of this break a conical peak lifts its head, flanked by two smaller elevations of similar shape. The earth, where the pines have left it bare, consists of patches of white and carmine, which, combined with the color of the cliffs, produce an extraordinary and very pretty effect. As we crossed the valley, the clouds, coursing in ragged shreds, fell lower and lower upon the hills, altering their outlines beyond recognition, and finally blotting them out altogether. But thus far we had only arrived at the portals of a city of marvels.

We followed a trail among great bowlders of sandstone on to a plain, the rain falling more heavily upon us, and our plodding horses sinking up to the knees in mud, until we came to a grove of pines, with dripping and glistening branches; and emerging from that we discovered a scene such as John might have dreamed of on Patmos—not of abnormal masses of rock tumbled together out of unshapely chaos, but the prospect of a fair city full of beautiful forms and colors. You can probably recall pictures of Italy in which all kinds of tints are pervaded by a golden haze that leaves them clear and brilliant, while reducing them to a degree of softness and mellowness like the wistful bluish-gray of a summer evening's sky. Think, then, of such a picture realized with all its subtilty of color; think of an amphitheatre of miraculous buildings, fanciful in form, and as fresh-looking as polished granite, composed of well-defined belts of mauve, violet, yellow, pink, gray, blue, and a score of other hues; think of Constantinople, or some other Oriental city, with its shabbiness weeded out, and only the palaces with the graceful minarets left; and from these thoughts you may gather an idea of the view that was disclosed to us as we came out of the pine grove.

First we saw a pyramid—a form which Nature seems especially fond of multiplying—200 feet high; at its base a shade of violet, which blends with an earthy brown that is next in the ribs of color surrounding it. Above these a line of carmine extends, melting into a soft rose-color, which by almost imperceptible degrees changes to a carmine again, and the apex is only reached by an infinite variety of the most astonishing chromatic transformations. Next, as we advanced, we saw a larger and more complicated structure, two towers connected by a wall in front, with an arrow-like spire midway between them; and for miles farther our interest was sustained by similar and no less picturesque rocks, some like crescent-shaped fortresses, others pointed and slim as needles.

others fairly round like water-batteries, and still others with the fretwork arches, the solid abutments and spires of great Gothic cathedrals.

In some places the stones have been eroded into thousands of little cells, like a worm-eaten piece of wood from the tropics; and occasionally a great split opens into a darksome cavern many feet deep. One of the strangest things about this strange region is its mutability. It is more or less changed every year; the soft clay that coats the sandstone is pitted with the prints of a million rain-drops, and the water in every little channel is as varicolored as the rocks themselves. You are amazed at the metamorphoses that a thousand years must have wrought, ever weaving fresh shapes and obliterating old ones out of this friable stone, while the main rocky range that is not far away has remained unaltered and immovable through all the ages.

Exactly at midday we reached the summit of the continental divide, the boundary separating the waters that flow into the Pacific from those that flow into the Atlantic, and that night we made a "dry" camp. It was technically called a "dry" camp, because it was far from any spring or river, but it was a very wet camp indeed to us. The rain that had fallen in torrents ceased as we pitched our tents on a sloppy mud bank, on which innumerable bear-tracks were imprinted; and toward 8 o'clock the welcome cry of "Supper!"

aroused at least one member of the expedition from melancholy reveries on lost comforts. But we had scarcely taken our seats at the frail table, improvised out of mess-chests, when a loud peal of thunder was heard overhead, and the next moment the rain came upon us with renewed force, driving us into our tents and thoroughly drenching our food, bedding, and clothing.

For five days following we had much to discourage us. Our water was gathered from the mud-puddles by the way, and remained as thick as gruel after four or five filtrations. The mules went thirsty and hungry. Little good grass could be found for them, and their backs broke into horrible sores in our long marches in search of pools. A fresh bone was visible in my mule's side for several mornings, and I am afraid to think how many ribs the unfortunate animal might have developed had we not soon found some fair grazing. But we had much to be thankful for, withal. Lieutenant Morrison's experience was of great advantage to us, and saved us from many sufferings and delays. We were fortunate, too, in striking the rainy season, which is distinguished from the dry season by a shower of about thirty minutes' duration every afternoon.

From the continental divide we traveled westward to the Cañon Blanco, which is inclosed by the same kind of rock and pliable clay as that which we had already seen in so many uncommon forms. A gritty yellow stone, exceedingly light in color, is also abundant, and is corroded into weird images like those in Monument Park, half suggestive of the preternatural and half suggestive of the preposterous. There is a notable tendency in much Western scenery to look like something artificial. Nature seems to be ever striving to dissemble, and make believe that her work is the work of man. In a branch of the Cañon Blanco we looked down upon a group of sandstones with a striking semblance to handsome modern buildings—one, for instance, rising by terraces to a cupola, each terrace being supported by regular lines of pillars. Next to this a crescent of pillars upholds a cornice, adorned by fretwork of extreme delicacy; and farther on a mass of stone counterfeits the old building of the Chicago Board of Trade. Some of the mesas, too, dissimilar from those seen in the earlier part of our journey, have bluffs formed by distinct rows of semicircular columns, which diminish in size from the base to the culminating point, and have the appearance of a rich mottled granite. The sturdy pines thrust themselves into the remotest nooks and corners, and find nutriment where no other living thing is seen.

It is related in an old legend that when the work of creation was finished the devil was filled with envy, and endeavored to produce another earth of his own design. He toiled and toiled with water, fire, and wind, and at last lifted volcanic Iceland, with its fells and jokulls, out of the sea. The same legend might be easily adapted to the country we explored beyond the Cañon Blanco, which is so completely desolate that not more than twenty whites have ever dared to enter it. It is a land without water, without game, or a single thing to sustain life—a blot on the fair earth, an irredeemable waste, indescribably dreary. Parts of it consist of alkali flats, without other vegetation than the intolerably pertinacious sagebrush, and parts of undulating plains, stretching monotonously for scores of miles. Hour after hour the mules plod through the valleys between the low knolls that divide the plains into troughs like the hollows of the sea, and hour after hour the vision is limited to the dull, gray walls of these abominable unvaried basins, which weigh down the mind and heart. Other parts consist of lava-beds, black with the crusted froth of extinct craters, and rugged with cliffs and caverns. But another part, consisting of alkali sand-dunes, is drier, hotter, and drearier than the flats or the plains. When the sun shines, as it often does with awful fierceness, the glaring whiteness of the sand almost blinds the traveler; and when the wind blows, as it often does with corresponding violence, the particles of dust flying in the air almost choke him. Sometimes, when a perfect calm prevails, a shrieking blast, as loud and harsh as a chorus of wolves, startles you from a reverie, and an instant afterward you are in the midst of a terrific whirlwind of sand and pebbles, which are carried thousands of feet into the air. I will not undertake to enumerate all the curses of this accursed country, however. To do so would be a greater tax on my Christian patience than my supply of that virtue will endure.

The course of a mean little creek, dignified into the name of Rio Chaco, straggles through the desert, filled at times with a sluggish mass of yellow mud; and this, with some pools, also muddy, afforded us the nearest approach to water we found in a march of seven days.

I have said that the country contains no game —that any one who should be lost would starve to death; but I ought not to omit mention of a thousand crawling things that infest it. Rattlesnakes are numerous enough to make us look carefully before each step; and a deadly species of the centipede, about five inches long and a quarter of an inch in diameter—a light, watery-looking reptile with black claws—has an aggressive way of insinuating itself among the bedding. Once in a while a coyote looks at you from behind a sage-bush, and runs away. A strange little flesh-colored insect, with big black eyes and a mouth altogether out of proportion to its other features, which the Mexicans call "Child of the Earth," on account of its grotesquely human appearance, is also seen. As for beetles that stand on their heads and wave their tails at you; beetles that dissolve themselves into a liquid which they squirt at you in their retreat; lizards large and small, swift and slow, plain and variegated in color—these are too common to call for notice.

Yet, all over this region, so worthless and deserted now, positive evidences are found that it was once populated by a civilized and numerous race, of whom the Pueblo Indians are possibly the descendants. On the banks of the Chaco, southwest of the Cañon Blanco, stands a magnificent ruin, named Pueblo Pintado, meaning in English Painted Town, of which three stories and cellars remain in an excellent state of preservation. I counted ninety-four separate rooms on the ground-floor alone, and there are signs of a fourth and possibly a fifth story. The walls measure from about one to three feet in breadth, and are built of solid blocks of stone, variable in size and hewed with the greatest nicety. The minutest crevice is filled, like a piece of mosaic work, with bits of stone that exactly fit it; and though little or no mortar has been used, this patchwork is as firm as a solid piece of rock. The exterior walls are formed of two thicknesses of stone, with a filling of adobe between, which gives them a breadth of nearly four feet, and renders them almost impregnable. The windows and doors open upon an interior courtyard, this arrangement evidently being part of a general plan of fortification ; and the courtyard contains several sunken chambers with circular walls marvelously perfect. No savant has ever determined positively to what race the occupants of this and the numerous similar ruins scattered over the country belonged. Neither whites nor Indians have any traditions concerning them, and only one thing is certain : that, whoever the builders were, they possessed a practical knowledge of the art of fortification and architecture, an amount of good taste and the means to gratify it, that entitle them to a high place in the scale of civilization.

Dr. Oscar Loew, who was attached to Lieutenant Wheeler's survey, thinks that New Mexico occupied a leading place among the few regions that were inhabited by civilized people on the discovery of this continent. All the Spanish records, though they are sometimes untrustworthy, agree as to the existence of a large number of inhabited towns in the territory—at least ten times the number of the present Pueblos. Some Spanish writers estimate the whole Pueblo population to have been fifty thousand ; and the cause of the decimation is probably traceable, in the first place, to the changes of climate that prompted emigration from certain parts of the country ; secondly, to the wars with the Spaniards ; and in the third place, to a mixture of the Spanish and Indian blood. Among the present Pueblos of New Mexico there is only one tradition in regard to the ruins. It is denied that they were depopulated by the Spanish wars, and it is said that the gradual decrease of the rainfall induced the inhabitants to emigrate to the south long before the Spaniards arrived in the country, being led by Montezuma, a powerful man who was born in Pecos, and who had settled with the Pueblos on the Rio San Juan. Montezuma was to return and lead the remaining Pueblos to the south, but he failed to come back. The Pueblos had been ordered by him to maintain the eternal fire, which is part of their religion; but generation after generation looked for him in vain, and now the fire is by no means perpetual.

The tradition agrees with another held by the Aztecs in Old Mexico when Cortes entered the country, namely, that their forefathers came (most probably at the end of the twelfth century) from the north; and their description of the country given to Cortes answers very well for New Mexico. Humboldt, without any knowledge of the existence of the ruins, supposed that the Aztecs came from the same part of North America. Some writers erroneously maintain that the Pueblos of New Mexico know nothing about Montezuma; but Dr. Loew asserts, on the contrary, that they have worshiped him next to the sun.

The fact that the Aztecs in Old Mexico had a monarchical government, while the Pueblos of

New Mexico are republican, is not considered an argument against the theory that the former came from New Mexico. The Aztecs might have confided their government to the family of Montezuma from feelings of gratitude or adoration. And the fact that the Aztecs in Old Mexico had some customs and a style of building different from the Pueblos of New Mexico, is not proof against the assertion, since the Aztecs on entering Old Mexico found tribes already there, with whom they mixed, and through whom they must have lost some of their original characteristics.

CHAPTER VIII.

OVER THE CHASKA MOUNTAINS TO FORT WINGATE.

Out of the Desert into a Paradise—The Navajo Reservation—The Amicability of the Tribe—An Old Chief's Idea of Whisky—The Giant's Armchair—Concerning several Interesting Members of the Camp—An Adventure at Albuquerque.

As we came out of the desert a line of mountains appeared against the horizon, which we knew to be the Chaska range. In the distance they did not promise much gratification to our wearied eyes ; but when we entered them by the

Washington Pass, a break about midway in the range, we were satiated with their beauties. The foliage is varied and luxuriant. Pines grow to a height of eighty feet, and the cottonwood forms itself into canopies, beneath the grateful shade of which the earth is carpeted with mosses and wild flowers in prodigious variety. There are Alpine bluebells of the tenderest blue ; roses, red, white, and yellow, of the most exquisite fragrance ; large buttercups and daisies that might have been wafted from English meadows ; purple-flowered morning-glories ; and a large delicate plant, which blossoms in three lavender-colored leaves mottled near the end, like the wings of a brown butterfly. We went over the foot-hills into the valleys, where gigantic bowlders lay wrapped in mosses and ferns, and through labyrinths of shrubs and trees, until we came to the mouth of the pass. Here we stood at the foot of a long, narrow slope of the brightest green grass, traversed by a brook that tumbled over several ledges in its descent. It was a natural clearing, with dense forests on each side ; and at the head, rising far above the giant pines, were two massive rock-towers, one of which we christened Niblack's Peak, out of compliment to the meteorologist of the party, a son of the Hon. William E. Niblack, of Indiana. Following the trail up and over the loose stones, we then reached a ravine where the foliage was thicker than ever, spreading and entangling itself into beautiful arches and festoons of branch and leaf. A little farther on was another clearing locked in by the walls of the pass, and in this primitive solitude we pitched our tents for the night.

We were now within the Navajo Indian reservation, and for several days were visited by many chiefs and squaws. The first wigwam we saw was built of boughs, twigs, and leaves. Two chiefs were taking their ease within on buffalo robes and wild-cat skins, while a pretty young squaw was busy weaving blankets. The two chiefs arose with smiling faces of welcome as we approached, and plied us with questions as to our experiences in the desert; but the little squaw scarcely raised her eyes, and hummed a strange little song as she hammered the wool down into her blanket. When the men had obtained some tobacco from us, they directed us to a trail; but we had not gone far when we heard the elder one calling after us. He soon overtook us, and told us that, as he was afraid we could not find water for the night's camp, he had decided to conduct us to it. In pursuance of his purpose he ran on before us out of breath, with beads of perspiration on his forehead, which he occasionally dried by taking a handful of loose soil and rubbing well over the skin. His dress was the same as that of all the Navajos, consisting of a cotton tunic gathered at the waist by a belt, with a simple leather bag attached, black cotton drawers, black cotton stockings, and yellow buckskin moccasins. His long black hair was tied into a cue, and a Turkey-red handkerchief was knotted across his brow. His face was frank and pleasant; his shoulders had great breadth, and his limbs were as supple as a cat's. He brought us to a pool of water, where he was joined by several other Indians, who left their work in the fields and rushed toward us the moment they saw us, remaining with us the whole evening, and watching with intense interest the work of unpacking the mules, putting up the tents, and cooking the supper. We, too, watched them with quite as great an interest, for the Navajos are dexterous, their consciences dull, and portable articles sometimes find their way from travelers' outfits into Navajo pockets in a way that will not bear explanation. But we lost nothing, and one by one our guests arose from the circle they had formed around our camp-fire, and, after wishing us good night, went home to their huts.

The Navajos number about eight thousand people, and have been for years on good terms with the whites. Many of them own farms and raise stock. During the time we were in their reservation they followed us from day to day, crowding about us while we were eating, and meddling with anything within their reach. Curiosity is a quality for which few give Indians credit, and the common idea of them is that they are stoical in disposition. But as a matter of fact they are like children in their inquisitiveness, and they insisted upon a close examination of our personal attire, the contents of our mess-chests, our arms, and our ammunition, not the smallest article escaping their notice. Speaking of this reminds me of an exceedingly amiable old chief who thrust his beaked nose into everything large enough to admit it. One of the men was sick, and went to the medicine-chest to get some pills, followed, of course, by the Indian. The long rows of little canisters and vials gave the old fellow great delight, and he took them in his hand one by one and smelled them with a varying expression on his face. At last he reached a bottle of concentrated ammonia, put it up to his nose, and inhaled heavily. The next moment he rolled over as if he had been shot, and for several seconds could neither breathe nor sneeze ; presently he recovered himself and shook his head. "No bueno ! no bueno !" he cried in Spanish ; "whisky no bueno !" and, as he was either tired of our company or ashamed of the undignified show he had made of himself, he went away, still sneezing, and we did not press him to stay.

We encamped in several Navajo villages which have some appearance of permanence. The houses are small, conical in shape, and built of logs, which are raised like a stack of muskets and covered with matting and sods. The squaws are industrious, and occupy themselves in weaving blankets, which are among the finest and most expensive made anywhere. Some of the wool is furnished by the Government, but the best white wool is made by themselves from their own sheep, and the finest red wool is made by picking cloth. Two or three hundred dollars each is not an unusual price for the large-sized blankets, which are waterproof and wonderfully warm.

Beyond the Washington Pass we entered Arizona by the way of Fort Defiance, and traveled for three days under the shadow of a line of red sandstone bluffs about eight hundred feet high, which are split in many places into detached needles. Here and there a volcanic mass rises alone from the plain, its black and porous substance covered with a yellowish-green moss; and among others we found one nearly a thousand feet high, to which Mr. Clark gave as a descriptive name "The Giant's Arm-chair." We continued to suffer for want of water, and when we arrived at Fort Wingate, several of our pack-mules were in so poor a condition that they could not have lived had we taken them farther. They were not only exhausted from overwork and want of food—a few days' rest would have cured them had that been all—but most of them were afflicted with festering sores worn in their sides by the pack-saddles or *aparajos*. For nearly three weeks their average marches had been of about ten hours' duration under an intensely hot sun each day, and during this time the load of each was not less than 150 pounds. Without good water or sufficient grass, with these heavy weights over their wounds, they trotted along briskly until the last day of their service, ascending and descending precipices on which no one unfamiliar with them would believe they could retain a foothold.

I thought at one time that a mule was a creature of no individuality ; that it differed from its fellows only in color and size ; and that its worst qualities were obstinacy and stupidity, and its best qualities patience and endurance. But my experience with the Wheeler Expedition taught me that, while a mule has the most fixed and silly opinions on some matters, it is usually sagacious, and has a distinct individuality. "Gray Johnny" was not much larger than a Shetland pony, and had an unconquerable temper, with a vicious way of showing it. One day, as we were ascending a cliff of sandstone clay by a narrow, slippery trail, he missed his footing and rolled fifty feet down an embankment, with over two hundred pounds of baggage on his back. He climbed up again unhurt, and had scarcely reached the path when he tumbled a second time, rolling over and over like a log. He struggled to the summit, however, and, evidently annoyed at his previous failures, he then kicked at the other mules, the trees, and the packers. When one of the latter went toward him with a lasso, to hold him while his pack was being readjusted, he snapped at the man's arm with his teeth, and, missing it, seized the rope and chewed it into a pulp. It thus appears that amiability was not one of Gray Johnny's virtues. He resented all familiarities with his heels, but he was an excellent worker; and when he broke down, from the effects of the Arizonian heats, too hard labor, and too poor food, we were all sorry to lose him.

Poor "Baby" was phenomenally quiet, and had all the symptoms of consumption or a broken heart. When her load was removed at the end of a long day's march, she would quickly retire to the shade of a pine-tree, without any of the antics played by her companions, and there she would stand aloof, with a pathetic look that went to my heart. The deceptive tricks and arts of which the other mules were guilty never entered her innocent head, and her virtues are affectionately cherished in the memory of all the members of the camp.

Very different from her, again, was the rawboned "Bismarck," a most crafty wretch, with an omnivorous appetite, which never seemed satisfied. Nothing within his reach was secure from his depredations, and at different times he robbed our mess of a whole ham, a bag of flour, a side of bacon, a box of tea, and several pounds of sugar. All things were to his taste, and when he could not get at the rations, he attempted to make as hearty a meal as possible of any articles of clothing left outside the tents. In this way he munched up a heavy coat, a woolen muffler, a pair of buckskin trousers, and a straw hat. We were awakened one night by the thud of hoofs, and discovered "Bismarck" vigorously kicking at the messchest, with a view apparently to consuming the contents. Finding that he was watched, he galloped away with a stolen package of tacks in his mouth, from the effects of which he deservedly suffered for several days. On another occasion two of the packers were issuing rations of molasses and flour, when they were interrupted by a call to supper. The moment their backs were turned, "Bismarck," who had been furtively watching them from a distance, stole up, and alternately dipped his nose into the bag of flour and the tub of molasses, until it was elongated to nearly twice its natural size. But gluttony was not his only vice. He poked his head into every door that happened to be opened in the settlements through which we passed, and was only prevented from entering by the size of his pack. At Santa Fé he walked into a wineshop, to the unspeakable dismay of the proprietor, who saw havoc among the glasses and bottles during his visit.

There is no stronger proof of animal sagacity than the quickness with which an inferior creature recognizes and puts itself under the leadership of one more intelligent. Among themselves the coyotes are timorous even when gathered in large numbers; but with a wolf at their head to guide them, they become dangerous foes. The mules, in the same way, put their trust in a horse, following it in places where they would not venture alone; and for this reason we had a bell-mare to lead the pack-train. We "hobbled" her at night, and it was then safe to let the mules run free, as they seldom wandered beyond the sound of her bell. But in every herd there are a few independent spirits, and "Bismarck" was one of these. He was not content to stray alone, however, and sometimes succeeded in alluring a few of his mates away from the safety of camp on a wild helter-skelter chase across the country. It was amusing to watch how cunningly he tempted them, first strolling as he nibbled the grass a short distance away from the bell-mare, and then looking up in a surprised way, that was meant to convey the impression that he had strayed unconsciously. When none of the others showed a disposition to join him, he would go no farther; but if he saw his manœuvres were watched, he would explain them by many furtive little motions, which were evidently intelligible to his companions. By such hints of possible freedom he sometimes induced a silly mule to follow him; but as a runaway nearly always returns toward the place he came from, we knew in what direction to seek him, and we invariably found him before he had traveled very far from camp.

I might describe each of the others as fully as I have described "Bismarck." I believe that it would be possible to write a novel of mule life, with a hero and heroine, a villain, and other characters to match those in the novels of our own society. But there are other points for mention of more practical interest.

The mule is unsurpassed for travel in wild mountain countries. It is tough, strong, patient, and sure-footed; and it is equally serviceable as a pack animal, a draught animal, or a riding animal. It is capable of traveling twenty miles a day, over rough mountain trails, for six months of the year, with a two-hundred-pound load on its back and a very small quantity of food in its stomach. On account of its varied usefulness, it is more highly valued than a horse in the far southwest, where an Indian pony is not worth more than sixty or eighty dollars, while a good mule is often not procurable for less than one hundred and twenty-five dollars. The pack-train of our expedition thus offered a strong temptation to the numerous cattle-thieves who infest such stock-raising countries as New Mexico; and we had to be watchful to avoid the unpleasant experience of awaking some morning and finding our animals "stampeded."

In the season of 1875 one of the surveying parties under Lieutenant Wheeler had a mishap of this kind, and the stolen mules were only recovered after a chase of four hundred miles over a rough country. If at the end of a day's march we could have stabled our animals, or tied them up, we should have been spared much uneasiness; but we carried no fodder with us, and were obliged to let them wander in search of the best grazing they could find near camp. We were singularly fortunate, however, and did not lose a single animal by theft until we arrived at Albuquerque. Here there is a corral, into which we turned our train at night, and here two of our best mules were stolen. About thirty miles farther up the Rio Grande is the little town of Algodones, which is known as a haunt of desperadoes and cattle-thieves; and thither Juan, our Mexican packer, was immediately dispatched. He was selected for the service in preference to an American, as his appearance in the town would excite less notice; and he sallied out of camp into the darkness, armed with a Springfield carbine, a Colt's revolver, and a liberal supply of cartridges, under orders to recover the mules if possible. He was away two days. Early the following morning Lieutenant Morrison started out in another direction, and discovered tracks of the missing animals in the loose dust of a frequently traveled road, some distance from camp. He recognized them by the fact that the prints showed a shoe missing from a hind hoof, and that one of the animals corresponded in this particular. He followed up this single clew for twenty-four hours, clearly tracing the hoof-prints along the road and over indistinct trails, where, to eyes less sharp than those of the Western path-finder, they would have been invisible. But at last he lost sight of them as they turned off into open country, and he came back to camp tired and disappointed. Juan returned the next day with no better luck, and we went away from Albuquerque poorer by two mules.

CHAPTER IX.

A COUNTRY FOR COLONIZATION.

A Geological Supper—What a Young Man might do in the Zuñi Mountains—Sheep-Farming in New Mexico—A Narrow Escape from Drowning in a Mud Spring—Emigrants from Indiana—All Night in a Mexican Ranch.

HAVING replaced our broken-down animals by others, our train presented a creditable appearance when we left Fort Wingate; and for the two weeks following our experiences were easy and pleasant—that is to say, we had plenty of good water and grass and short marches. Bacon for breakfast, bacon for lunch, and bacon for supper, is not in itself a thing calculated to fulfill one's ideas of an agreeable and nutritious article of diet. If our rations had been supplemented by a little fresh meat, or if ever that most frugal of vegetables, a potato, had been added to them, we should have been immeasurably nearer the ordinary standard of comfort. But fresh meat was only accessible to the expedition about once in three weeks; fruit only grows in the valley of the Rio Grande; and potatoes are as scarce as pomegranates in Greenland. Still, compared with what we had passed through, our experiences were absolutely luxurious.

For several weeks the rain was more frequent than before; and had we not been profoundly grateful for it, and fully sensible of the refreshing humidity and coolness produced in the atmosphere, we might have complained of the precipitate manner it had of coming down and surprising us. Several times, when the afternoon was serene and clear, when our benevolent cook had spread the table-cloth and prepared all things for supper —baked bread and fried pork—the pines around our camp suddenly began to moan and crackle, and the cottonwoods to tremble as with a palsy. Following these signs, great storm-clouds with hurricane folds raced across the heavens, and within a few moments the sky was hidden in murky vapors that dissolved in torrents over our unlucky heads. On such occasions all ceremonies were dispensed

A COUNTRY FOR COLONIZATION. 115

with; a rush was made on the table, and each man seized the dish nearest to his hand, disappeared with it into his tent, and made as satisfying a meal of it as he could, whether it consisted entirely of condiments, bread, or vegetables. As for me, I was usually fortunate enough to secure a variety of dishes on one plate, and, upon arriving at my tent in one of these sudden storms, found myself the happy possessor of a geological sort of mess, made up, so to speak, of several different periods. The upper crust consisted of dried apples, and beneath this was a stratum of baked beans, in which a small fossilized tree in the shape of a pickled cauliflower was imbedded. Exploring further, and with increasing interest, I unearthed some doughy bread permeated with bacon gravy, and a teaspoonful of sugar evidently deposited in the wrong place during the confusion of the moment. "Be bold; ever be bold; be not too bold." I had seen enough. I was hungry, and did not dare to go farther. My knife was without a fork and my tea without sugar. The rain had accumulated in the bottom of my plate, and was beating against the edges of the food; but I was hungry, and I relished my supper heartily. For the rest of the evening I smoked my pipe, and, wrapped in an Ulster overcoat, lay in my tent reading the last newspaper that had come to hand, while the rain pattered dismally on the outside.

A march of twelve miles from Wingate brought

us to Bacon Springs, along a road skirting on one side a line of sandstone bluffs, a light red in color, which extended east and west a distance of over forty miles. The general form of these rocks is that of palisades, unbroken by crag or buttress from their summits to their bases; but in several places they throw capes, with flat tops and columnar sides, far out into the plains that gird them. On the other side of the road are the Zuñi Mountains, which, compared with some of the ranges that we have occupied, are mere foothills, and do not in any place attain a greater height than 8,200 feet. But what they lack in eminence is compensated for by a fertile soil and luxuriant vegetation. An Eastern farmer would probably doubt the veracity of a person telling him of the existence in New Mexico of a grass so palatable that animals choose it in preference to clover. But in the lovely valleys of these mountains, where the purple blossoms of this plant load the air with their honeyed fragrance, there is a species of bunch grass, both nutritious and wholesome, of which the statement is quite true—a grass growing in abundance over hundreds of acres in wavy plumes a foot high.

I think there are few places in the Territory where the aspect is so promising that an educated young man familiar with the Eastern States would be content to settle had he any other object than pecuniary gain, or where, even though he invested his patrimony, he could be induced to remain and attend to his interests. I have very little sympathy with those colonization schemes that would suddenly transplant a boy from the lap of luxury to a Kansas flat, and there bid him exhaust his energies in irrigating a wilderness. But in the Zuñi Mountains there is splendid grazing, a rich soil, and plenty of good spring-water. The valleys are gardens. Our trail was curtained in places by a sort of sunflower growing to a height of eight feet, and acre after acre was covered with blossoms, some like rubies with a golden fringe, others a gorgeous scarlet, others—but it is useless to attempt an enumeration of the prodigal displays of color that we met everywhere in this fertile country. The forests abound with game. For three days the bacon in our mess was superseded by venison cutlets, breaded, and venison stew. One afternoon Mr. Karl entered camp from the mountains in a state of extreme excitement. He had seen two bears within an hour of each other. On the next day Lieutenant Morrison saw a third bear, two herds of elk, and several flocks of wild turkeys besides ; but as neither gentleman had his gun with him at the time, and as it is a thankless task to throw stones at either turkey or deer, and especially thankless to trifle unarmed with a bear, we were soon doomed to bacon again.

A young man might settle here with all conditions in his favor. He might build himself a ranch, and learn to be happy among picturesque scenery and in a bracing climate. With a thousand dollars he could purchase a fairly stocked sheep farm. His flock would not, of course, appear very imposing by the side of those of the wealthy Mexicans, some of whom have nearly a quarter of a million sheep; but he would grow in self-respect and courage as he stood at the door of his ranch after a day's work, and saw visible evidence that he was really doing something in the world.

The lands are public, and some speculators with very easy consciences are fast absorbing them by preëmption. During a day's march through some of the most beautiful valleys, we saw how this generous law is complied with, or, I should say, how it is infringed. For a dwelling an empty log hut entirely open on one side—this for the door and window—is built, and a few branches are thrown over it for a roof. The "actual residence" consists in an occasional visit by the preëmptor, whose conscience would not otherwise allow him to swear that he had lived on the land for the prescribed time.

But while the Zuñi Mountains are so fertile, they are bounded by desolate plains and mesas, and the traveler who seeks them has many hardships to endure before he reaches them. Occasionally, when we were near a road, we found the sandstone bluffs engraved and penciled with the names of those who had preceded us, and under the travelers' autographs there was sometimes a brief criticism of the country. One had cut his name in letters an inch long on one bluff, with the date of his passing, and a commentary : "This is a —— of a place. August, 1864." Another wayfarer, coming several years later, has let a little light upon his experiences by writing sympathetically under the previous legend : "Right you are, by thunder !" No effort of the imagination is needed in those who have learned the toilsomeness of a long day's march over barren plains to realize the disgust that these two sufferers had felt in camping by an alkali spring, the waters of which were bitter to the taste and aggravating to the thirst.

Mr. Clark again left the main party at Bacon Springs to go on a side trip, and was absent five days, returning with a crust of bread, the last morsel of his rations, after some pretty rough experiences. On the following morning he started out with a packer on another excursion, and was instructed to join us at a point above Agua Fria in the evening. In order to find good grass and water, we went several miles farther than we intended, however, and evening came without Mr. Clark. A large fire was lighted and kept burning brightly all night, but the topographer was still missing—a circumstance the more distressing since the rain fell in torrents. No one doubted his safety, but all were concerned for his comfort, and had an opportunity of expressing their sympathy in the morning, when he rode into camp with his companion, hungry and wet to the skin. He had been detained on a neighboring peak, and on getting down was overtaken by darkness, which prevented him from finding our trail. There was not a ranch within ten miles, and he spent the stormy and sleepless night seated in a pine forest, where the lightning shattered trees within a few feet of him. A week or two before he narrowly escaped drowning in a mud-spring. He noticed what seemed to be a patch of moisture a few yards from the trail, and as we were short of water he dismounted from his horse to examine it. Stretching out his toe in the gracefully cautious manner of a nymph trying the water before bathing, his foot sank from under him, and in less time than it takes to write these words, as the authors of the "penny dreadfuls" say, he was up to his knees in mud. He recovered himself by a vigorous leap, and had the satisfaction of discovering by fathoming the spring, which was over twelve feet deep, that he had escaped death of a horrible kind.

Few people visit New Mexico for pleasure. The travelers from the East that we occasionally met were all bound on errands of business among the miners, stock-raisers, and Indians. One day we encountered two families from Indiana, who had first migrated to Colorado Springs, and, not having succeeded there, were bound to Arizona, whence, in event of another failure, they proposed to go to Southern California, and home again to the old farm, by the Wabash, should all things turn against them. Apparently they had quite forgotten that man's life is limited to three score and ten, and they looked forward to all possible reverses with cheerful resignation, and a degree of confidence in their own recuperative powers that was fairly sublime. The elders were not beginners in the battle either, as their faded appearance proved. It did not seem possible that the lank, cadaverous men had enough virility in them to go through with any undertaking. The women were tall, thin, shrill, flat-breasted, and sharp-eyed. There were some very young girls among them, and I thought that they too would be haggard and gray before the strife was over. But all the members of the party were lively and energetic in their conversation, and, in alluding to their unsettled condition and their uncertainty of achieving anything, were apparently as content as though they were on the road to certain riches.

A greater drawback to the Territory than the thriftlessness of its native inhabitants is the lack of transportation facilities. Between the principal towns there are stage-lines, with small, uncomfortable coaches, that travel night and day at the rate of about six miles an hour. The fare of these conveyances is twenty or twenty-five cents a mile, and only forty pounds of baggage are allowed to each passenger. A light, uncovered wagon called a "buckboard" is run with the mail between less important points, and the fare by this is the same as by coach. Meals at the stage stations cost one dollar each ; and, if the traveler finds it necessary to "put up" at a native ranch, he is sometimes charged still more exorbitantly. One evening two belated members of our party were away from camp on a side-trip, and, having neither food nor bedding with them, sought lodgings at the ranch of a Mexican. They were supplied with a supper of chicken, bread, and coffee. As is the custom, one of the women of the house then asked them whether they would prefer to sleep indoors or out ; and, as the night was damp, they selected the inside. So two mattresses and blankets were spread for them on the floor of the sitting-room, and they prepared to retire. The bashful young German professor, who rode the odometer of the expedition, was unbuttoning his coat, when his sunburnt face became overspread with blushes. The host and hostess were making two extra beds on the other side of the room ; and before the young Teuton could recover his composure they had blown out the lamp, and tucked themselves in. But this was not the worst. Señora had a bad toothache, and Señor constantly muttered quiet oaths all to himself.

Two more sympathetic men do not breathe than the guests; but what wonder that this dismal concert awoke vengeful feelings in them, as they tossed uneasily in their beds? In the midst of the night Señor rose stealthily and went out of the room. By and by he returned and stood at the entrance, looking in a commiserating way at the explorers, one of whom lay awake, wondering what the old fellow meant. Presently Señor said, in the placid voice of a person conveying some good news : " One of the mules has gone "— one of the mules that had been intrusted to his care the night before! *El diablo!* The guests were up in a moment and outside the house in the darkness. Señor followed leisurely with an undisturbed face, puffing at a cigarette with as little concern as a bee has for the wind that rocks the stalk on which it rests. He looked calmly around from the doorway while his guests were tearing their feet to pieces on the rocky hill-sides, and anon he espied the missing brute grazing near the corral. "See," he says, "there it is." And when he is reviled he replies with the greatest equanimity, " *Hablemos de otra cosa, Señores* " —let us change the subject. In the morning the guests made a frugal breakfast of jerked beef, bread, and coffee, and called for their score. The old sinner had the impudence to demand five dollars, to insist upon it, and to swear by all the saints in the calendar that his prices were ruinously low.

CHAPTER X.

A MODERN PUEBLO.

Peeping into a Crater—The Wonders at the Bottom—Traveling over a Lava Bed—The Settlement of Laguna—The Dress and Personal Appearance of the Pueblo Indians—Madame Pueblo—Old Palestine Reproduced—A Pastoral Community—The Pharisaism of the Missionaries—The Chasm in the Plain—The Fertility of the Bottom Lands of the Rio Grande.

By consulting a map the reader will see that after leaving Pueblo, we worked in a partial circle around Santa Fé. At Tierra Amarilla the former town was one hundred miles distant; at Fort Wingate it was one hundred and fifty miles distant; and we were not at any time more than three hundred miles away from it, although the distance traveled measured over one thousand miles. At Wingate the main division had done six hundred and thirty-five miles, and the side parties one hundred and thirty-five miles. After that we traveled, with détours, nearly three hundred miles more.

The previous chapters have shown that our path was not altogether easy. For several days before reaching Albuquerque our rations were reduced to coffee without sugar, and dry bread.

We made dinners of herbs, and tantalized our thirst with mud. But we read in nearly every page of Nature's book, and saw her infinitely manifest in the sterile plains, the gorgeous mesas, and the snowy sierras of the Mother Range.

To the earnest geologist, more than to any other man, she has revealed herself in New Mexico ; and she speaks to him here in her various tones with an eloquence that compensates him for all the annoyances incident to camp-life in a desert. As if to complete our experiences so as to include in them every note that composes her scale, we found a little to the west of Agua Fria, among the Zuñi Mountains, a crater as perfect as it was twenty-four hours after its last volume of hissing flame. As we looked at it from the distance, it was simply one peak in a chain of hills, well robed in foliage ; but as we ascended it with a view to establishing a triangulation station on the summit, and passed over the timber-line, we found masses of broken lava before us, in which our feet sank ankle-deep. The bubble-blown ashes of the earth's dead passions were covered with lacerating points like nails that double-soled boots could no more resist than a sheet of paper. But we toiled on and on, dragging ourselves up by projecting stones and bunches of grass. Below us were the pines and the clearings, yellow and purple with sunflowers and clover. Looking up, we seemed to be climbing the sides of an inverted basin, the bottom of which was represented by the flat top of the peak.

When we had climbed eight hundred or nine hundred feet above the surrounding level, we gained the summit, and stood on a rim of black lava, which extended about four feet inwardly around the cone. This was the lip of the crater, and advancing to the edge of it, we looked into the throat. A whole week's toil would have been repaid in the sight that met us—a sight so novel and beautiful that, remembering it, any one would be ready to think only of the grand features of New Mexico. The abyss was not dark, although its great depth was proved by the distant sound of pebbles that we threw into it. By the same process that it gives color to the flowers, the sun seemed to have shed some of its warm splendors on the corrugated mass of lava, which was lighted with bands of yellow and red, joining each other by a hundred intermediate tints. I can give no idea of how rich these colors were, nor can I describe how the crimson faded into a faint pink, and how the yellow, in its fullness a buff, was transmitted by various shades into a delicate amber-tint, like the confession of dawn in the morning sky. I can only tell how the members of the expedition, breathless from their exertions, stood on the brink of the hollow, full of silent amazement and rapture. But the colors were not all. Blown into the air by a strong wind, some cottonwood seeds had dropped into the crater, and grown out of its rocky heart into mature trees, with canopies of quivering leaves and silvery boughs. Their highest branches were at least seventy feet below us; and as the wind swept among them, the concave walls echoed the murmurs, until it sounded like the chorus of a great forest in a gale.

The country to the west was fair, with hills and valleys, and to the north mesas gleamed red and white and green. But toward the south there was a sea of lava rolling over many miles, unrelieved by a blade of grass or a single tree. Over a large area east of the Zuñi Mountains similar volcanic remains are seen in a multitude of forms—sometimes in great blocks piled one over the other along the banks of a stream, and sometimes in crumbling walls and oval shells, lying among verdant fields.

Between Agua Fria and the Mexican town of San Rafael, which is near the former site of Fort Wingate, we saw a number of small craters from ten to fifty feet high, climbing which we looked into deep caverns extending far below the surface. These are completely coated by moss, and are so hedged in by greenery that they lend an additional charm to the scene. Some one has spoken of Edinburgh Castle as a lump of verdigris—a simile neither poetic nor elegant, but graphic, and one that describes the volcanic fragments better than I can. They look very much like romantic old English abbeys sequestered among patriarchal yews and tenacious ivy.

But the black plain that we saw from the summit of the principal crater had not one beauty to gladden the eye. It was a forbidding waste, and those members of the expedition who ventured to cross it nearly came to a disastrous end. The spikes in the surface tore off their mules' shoes, and wore their hoofs to the bone. For several miles their path had been trailed in blood, and when they came into camp they had been afoot forty-eight hours. The mules, which were the finest animals in our herd, subsequently died.

Soon after we left the Zuñi range, Mount Taylor, or the Mountain of San Mateo, as it is variably called, came into view, and for several days we saw its three peaks high above the mesas—in the early morning, when they were cold and wreathed in clouds; at sunrise, when long rays of light fell upon them and illuminated their knolls and cliffs; and in the evenings, when they glowed for a moment before a heavy haze of blue flooded them like a rising tide, and closed them in its folds for the night. They were landmarks to us for many weeks. We first caught a glimpse of them when we were on the Mesa Tachada, again near the Zuñi Mountains, and again near Santa Fé. The highest measures about thirteen thousand feet above the level of the sea, and this, with the others, which are almost the same height, is visible from every important elevation in the Territory.

Traveling in an eastern direction from Agua Fria to Albuquerque, we stayed for a day near the Indian settlement of Laguna, one of the modern pueblos. The old ruins, such as Pueblo Pintado, are much superior as works of architecture to the modern towns, and the movement of their race, if we assume that the old and new dwellers in the pueblos come of the same stock, has been retrograde. But the Pueblo Indians of to-day, deteriorated as they are, rank in all respects as far above the savage Comanches, Cheyennes, and Arapahoes of the plains, and the sneaking Utes and Apaches of the mountains, as the comely, lovable natives of the Society Islands rank above the cannibals who live on the same archipelago within a few hundred miles of them.

The men dress like the Navajos. They wear a girded tunic of some cotton print, usually figured with flowers, and sometimes made of two Turkey-red pocket handkerchiefs. Their legs are sheltered in cotton drawers and a breech-clout; or I should say parts of their legs are sheltered in this way, for these children of nature have so curtailed their drawers that their presence might cause a very bashful person much embarrassment. Their long, wiry hair is gathered behind in a cue, and tied by a ribbon, a string, a slip of buckskin, or a

9

shoe-lace. The red pocket handkerchief again comes into service as a tiara, and when we have mentioned this, with the breech-clout, the tunic, a bead-work shot-bag, and a powderhorn, we have completely enumerated all the important features of a Pueblo Indian's outfit. They are not as handsome as the Navajos, and do not look as powerful. Their bodies are spare and their faces wan. Judging them by their appearance, you would consider them sad, but they are as light-hearted as children.

The women are short and broad, and like great rag dolls, so extensively are they swathed in clothes. The bandages begin at the ankles and continue, in one form or other, almost without intermission, to the neck. Madame Pueblo indulges in a few barbarian colors. Her dress is usually black, the funereal tone of which is enlivened by a red tippet. She is not in the condition of abject submission to her husband that the women of other tribes are. Her lord and master graciously condescends to carry the baby sometimes; and, if he has been to school, he assists in the rougher household duties, such, for instance, as bringing home the melons for dinner, and chopping wood for the fire. We saw a woman surrounded by her pretty children in the Navajo country, felling pines with a heavy axe, and not resting from her work once in an hour, while her stalwart husband stood by and watched the sweat rolling from her. But where there are American schools, as in the pueblos, the women are treated with a little kindness; and it is a pity that the zealous reformers in the States who are so anxious to emancipate contented young wives from the thraldom of loving husbands do not divert some of their superfluous energy toward the establishment of more schools among the Indians, in which good work they might find a practical reward. Whenever we encamped near an Indian settlement, the inhabitants came down to see us, and showed a child-like delight and interest in our outfit. The men crowded around the theodolite, unable to make out whether it was a pepper-box or a new kind of weapon; and if the topographer was in a conceding mood, they, to their intense satisfaction, were permitted to peep through it. Among the Navajos the squaws meanwhile sat at a respectful distance, naturally dying of curiosity, which they, poor things, dared not gratify by approaching nearer. But the Pueblo "bucks" were more gallant, and, when they had exhausted all the wonders themselves, they generously gave their wives a chance to take one peep before going home. This was a real triumph of education over selfishness and brutality, and we commend it to the consideration of those agitators who, in a paradox, are only content in their discontent.

The houses of the Pueblo Indians, as I have

already explained, are built of adobe in terraces, on a commanding hillside, and in their original condition of fortification were only accessible by a portable ladder. The occupants of the lower story still use this primitive device, from necessity rather than fear or desire ; but in these good days of peace the ladders are never removed, the lower stories are supplied with doors and windows, and the stranger passes through the city gates unmolested and unquestioned. Each tenement consists of two or three rooms, and outside each terrace there are several dome-shaped mud ovens, four or five feet high, which are used in common. The floors are of mud, the walls are of mud, and the roofs are of logs. There is nothing of the picturesque in the prevailing squalor and dilapidation of the houses. They scarcely seem fit for occupancy, so ruinous are they. A chair or a table is an unwonted luxury, and a sign of its owner's wealth. But the manners and dress of the Indians—the black-robed women with water *ollas* balanced on their heads, and the long-haired men in their loose tunics driving ox-teams or shouldering primitive scythes—give an oriental aspect to the winding, ill-conditioned little streets within the walls.

There is a strong resemblance between some of the features of New Mexican villages and old Palestine, as it is pictured in the Bible. The likeness is strongest among the simple dwellers in the pueblos, who are industrious and care little for the pleasures of the chase. Their farms, acquired in old Spanish grants, include some of the best land in the Territory, and are cultivated with greater care and better results than those of the neighboring Mexicans. Their principal crops are maize, wheat, apples, and (in the valley of the Rio Grande) grapes, plums, and melons. A bowery lookout is built of interlaced boughs in every field, and soon after sunrise the women and children issue from their houses, and make their way to their own patches, where, sheltered in one of the summer-houses, they remain guarding the crops from thieves during the day. I question if there is a happier people under the sun than these wild children, to whom life seems to be one long, sunny summer, without a troublesome cloud of jealousy, anxiety, or hatred. Laughter ripples among the leaves the whole day. The women love their babies with passionate devotion, and in this respect are as good and kind as the best of white mothers; and the children scarcely ever quarrel, the older ones showing the younger ones a degree of forbearance that would be eminently creditable to young Christians were it a little more frequent among them. Meanwhile the men are at work in the fields with clumsy wooden plows, drawn by lazy ox-teams; and when evening comes, and the laborers prepare to start for home, one of their number is detailed to remain in the lookout bower, where his voice is heard during the night rising in the strange, plaintive song of his people.

It is lamentable that the religious dissensions of sects which bring missionary endeavor to ridicule in nearly every part of the world have even broken out in these quiet, out-of-the-way little pueblos. In this settlement of Laguna I have been describing, there is a humble little adobe building with a belfry, where a Catholic priest officiates once a month, and a similar building that is used conjointly by a Protestant minister and a government schoolmaster. The twelve hundred Indians in the town might learn many lessons in grace and arithmetic were their instructors united ; but the minister and dominie are alienated from the priest on spiritual grounds, while he is opposed to them in all things. The Roman Archbishop has openly declared his antagonism to unsectarian schools, and discourages the attendance of his parishioners in them. So the little mud church, instead of being a monument of paternal love and wisdom, is an element of discord and enmity ; and it might have been better for the people had they been left to develop their spiritual natures in the glow of heathen fires rather than be converted to a religion so perverted from its truth by the prejudices of its ministers that it teaches Pharisaism in its first lessons. A part of the inhabitants still believe in the coming of Montezuma, and worship in subterranean chambers, into which foreigners are seldom admitted. Complete secrecy in their ceremonies is considered so essential that guards are posted at the entrance to the town several times in the year ; but these are the only occasions when the prying stranger is refused admittance to the streets.

About twenty miles from Laguna we crossed some plains near Sheep Spring, and suddenly came upon a deep volcanic ravine, with walls of bluish lava, sheer from the top to the bottom, and at least seven hundred feet high. In running over the continent by railroad, while under the influence of the monotonous character of the plains and prairies, one is inclined to think that, compared with the latter, the proportion of picturesque scenery in America is insignificant. But before one has traveled many hundred miles in New Mexico or Colorado, he is bound to acknowledge that any one of their abounding marvels would be enough to make a more accessible country famous. What has the East, or England, or France, or Germany to equal this ravine, for instance, the Cañado Alamos, as it is called ? Compared with it, the Pictured Rocks, the Virginia Natural Bridge, Watkins Glen, or the most curious features of the British coast are worth as little note as a boy's box of magic compared with the best tricks of a skilled prestidigitateur ; and yet here, in the midst of a thousand marvels, it has nothing more than a name and scarcely excites a moment's wonder. The surrounding country is almost flat, and is bounded by abrupt mesas. We march along with apparently nothing but the plains ahead of us, and suddenly, without warning, as we approach a crest of the wavy land, we see the edge of the gulf. Less than a dozen yards away this enormous fissure lays bare the earth in a width of two hundred feet and a depth of seven hundred feet. The walls are plumb and smooth, the color of coal. The flat bottom is filled with yellow sand and pebbles, meandered by a babbling creek. Thickets of trees and shrubs crop out of all this barrenness, apparently independent of nourishment; and here a great slice of lava leans over from the farther wall, as though it had been cut by a knife, only awaiting an occasion to tumble into the cañon. In the chasm between it and the mainland a forest is growing; and as we throw stones down it, a flock of birds shriek remonstrance at our unprovoked assault.

From this point we struck for the fertile valley of the Rio Grande, the most productive part of New Mexico, and in a week reached the odd little town of Santa Fé.

The bottom lands of the Rio Grande with which we became acquainted have been compared to the Nile, of Egypt; and they form the best portion of New Mexico, in an agricultural point of view. Four fifths of the population live upon the banks of the Rio Grande, and the settlements are traversed by large irrigating ditches, averaging two feet in depth and three in width. The river carries with it large quantities of a reddish-gray matter, which settles when the water is left in repose for several hours ; and this is the only fertilizer used, the soil yielding fruits, grain, and farm-produce of every description in abundance, notwithstanding the fact that it has been under cultivation for over two hundred and fifty years. Onions weighing over two pounds, cabbages of sixty pounds, turnips of enormous size, peas, watermelons, squashes, beans, Indian corn, and figs are grown in great profusion.

The bottom lands appear well adapted to grape-growing, and already the El Paso wine has gained a great reputation. It was said that, although every effort had been made to raise potatoes, none had been successful. But the cause of the failure was ascertained to be carelessness on the part of the Mexicans, who neither hoe the ground sufficiently nor remove the numerous caterpillars from the herbage ; and more intelligent Americans have succeeded in raising potatoes of fine quality.

While the properties of these lands are so excellent, however, the bottoms do not average more than two miles in width, and the mesas embracing them show hardly a sign of vegetation, excepting the sage-bush. Wherever water does not border the soil, or is not carried there by ditches, even grass is absent, and vegetation is defeated by the scarcity of rains, combined with the sandy, porous nature of the soil. Well-watered ground and a perpetually dry atmosphere form a union of circumstances exceedingly favorable for splendid development of crops of all kinds. This fact can be observed not only in New Mexico along the valleys of the water-courses, but also in Colorado, where by means of irrigation the most abundant crops are developed. In 1872 three times as much corn was raised to the acre in Colorado as in neighboring Kansas, where a moist atmosphere and occasional rains obviate the necessity of irrigation. The splendid growth of firs and pines above an altitude of 7,000 feet in New Mexico may also be attributed to the above-mentioned facts. The soil contains sufficient moisture for the trees, while the atmosphere is mostly dry and the sky seldom covered with clouds. Thus the reduction of carbonic acid is rarely retarded by absence of direct sunlight; the circulation of the sap is greatly increased by the more rapid evaporation from the leaves; and all moisture necessary for the body of the tree is supplied by the roots.

CHAPTER XI.

SANTA FÉ.

The Capital of New Mexico—The Modesty of the Señoras—The Appearance of the Streets—A Very Mixed Population—The Attractions of a Baby Carriage—Croquet in the Mountains—Scenes around a Gambling Table—The Great Army Game of " Chuck-a-Luck "—A Mexican Ball.

WHEN one is traveling toward an objective point for three consecutive months, it is bound to excite some speculations on its appearance, whether it be Rome, Reykjavik, Paris, or Pottsville; and those members of the expedition to whom the Territory was a new country looked forward to our arrival at Santa Fé with greater interest than our actual acquaintance with the town sustained. Santa Fé is the axis on which New Mexico turns, the capital of the Territory, and the distributing point of all the territorial mails. It was a rising settlement when the progenitors of the St. Nicholas Society first possessed Manhattan Island, and it is as iniquitous as it is old. It has political rings, show-windows, and bar-rooms; and we looked forward to it as a restoration to the luxurious civilization that we left behind at Pueblo. But our speculations as to its appearance were all wrong, as such speculations usually are. We reached it from the town of Galisteo, twenty-two miles away, traveling through an undulating country, wooded by sturdy cacti, three or four feet high, and knots of dwarf pine. Toward three in the afternoon we attained the crest of a hill, and in the valley below lay Santa Fé, sunning itself by the side of a great mountain.

It is not an impressive little city by any means, but it is compactly built, and has not the erratic inclination of many Mexican towns to straggle over as much ground as possible. We entered by a long, narrow street lined with one-storied mud houses, mostly built in the form of quadrangles, with interior courtyards, suggestive of small model prisons. Some dark-eyed señoras and señoritas were seated at the doors making cigarettes, and they drew their shawls more closely about them as we passed. A glance into the interior of the houses showed us clean mud floors and whitewashed mud walls, with the family couch rolled up to do service for chairs during the day. Had we come along here in early morning, we should have found this part of the population abed in the street; for these warm-blooded Southerners seldom sleep indoors during the hot weather. The black shawls were closing like so many crows' wings as we advanced. Indeed, the Mexican woman is strangely coy with this article of dress, which she uses as a substitute for both mantle and bonnet; and, however short or long a distance she is going, she never fails to throw it over her head, sometimes in such a way as to conceal the whole of her lower features. Shoes and stockings, bare legs and feet, are matters of indifference to her, but she is ever scrupulous about the *tapalo*. Some drunken soldiers put their beery faces outside a door to stare at us, and a Pueblo Indian trotted along on a donkey or burro ahead of us, seated so far astern that we thought he must have been brought up to ride on the tail itself in case of necessity. Then an eight-bull wagon team blocked the way, and its Mexican drivers hissed and spluttered blasphemy.

Thus far we had not seen an American, and all things looked foreign to us. The cramped cobble-stoned streets, with their hedges of squat flat-roofed houses; the porticoes reaching from every house to the curb; the brown passers-by, with bushy black hair and lustrous eyes; the indescribable frowsy hucksters seated at the corners before their scant stocks of watermelons— these were Mexican elements. But by and by we passed from the outskirts into the busy part of the town, which is comprised within the space of a small square, with a leafy little park in the center, and here we were at the very core of the Territory.

With two exceptions, the stores are all one story high, and a barber's pole is the only ornament among them all; but they run backward and sideward to such an extent that they manage to cover considerable space. The north side of the square is occupied by the Governor's "Palace," which is an oblong adobe, completely uninteresting and unimaginably ugly. In fact, the people of Santa Fé seem utterly destitute of taste, and out of all the merchants, many of whom are very wealthy, not one has built a pretty store or house for himself. In the park there is a soldiers' monument. It is an obelisk, and it shows how ungraceful so simple a form as that may be made by unskillful hands. The sculptor's name is McGee, and he is welcome to the fame of his work. Quite an active throng circulates on the plaza—fashionably dressed civilians, military officers in blue and gold, rough-looking soldiers, weather-beaten emigrants, and broad-hatted teamsters with raw-hide whips that they crack like a pistol. There is a clanking of spurs on the sidewalk, and some dashing cavalrymen clatter round the corner. A baby carriage comes along; and what balm, what bliss, what consolation, what visions of all kinds of tender emotions and scenes that baby carriage, with its fair propeller, neatly dressed in bewitching muslin, gave to us vagabonds who had been so long removed from all domesticity! I never cared about these perambulators before, and regarded them somewhat in the light of a nuisance to an active pedestrian. But I am at a loss for similes to describe how grateful this little vehicle was. It was like the verbena in the dry mesa country, like all the especially pleasant things I can think of—like a cup of French coffee after a good dinner, or like the smoke of a favorite meerschaum after a hard day's work. There were some very handsome and tastefully dressed children afoot also, with very natty nursery maids in attendance; and we began to think better of Santa Fé. Our good opinion was fairly won when we saw the officers' quarters, a row of pretty little cottages set in gardens among trees, their wide porticoes walled with a bowery wall of trailing plants running from top to bottom. The flowers hedged them in on every side—flowers of every color and many shapes. Some of the windows are curtained with damask and lace, and the interiors are furnished with a degree of luxury and taste quite unusual in this savage Western world. In the evenings the band plays and the ladies engage in croquet. Then, if you are a looker-on and see the purple fall on the mountain opposite, and hear the beat of the mallets and the strain of the music, the effect is very pretty.

We camped in front of the new court-house, the building of which was begun twelve years ago, and has not yet been finished. What there is of it consists of four walls of stone, without any ornamentation, and a number of windows with wooden frames in them, and these together cost $70,000.

Let us glance now at the night side of the town. The streets are well filled, for the Santa Féan is an inveterate prowler, and invariably sallies forth after dark to "see what is going on." There is some strumming music in the saloons, and if your ears are sharp you may catch the sound of the dice-box, and hear such monosyllables as "tray, two aces, deuce, and a four." Here is a place called the Bank Exchange, which is ruffled all over with tissue-paper frills that cover ceilings, walls, and bar. Three musicians are seated in an alcove at the back, which is also ruffled with tissue paper, one with a cornet, another with a guitar, and the third with a flageolet. The cornet might as well be alone, for its windy efforts completely swamp the other two instruments. The floor is occupied by about six gaming-tables, each of which is presided over by a banker and surrounded by a crowd of men and boys. The greatest number, however, swarm around a table the master of which might stand for a portrait of Mr. John Oakhurst, of Poker Flat. The game here is "chuck-a-luck," and is described through the nose as "the old army sport played all the way from Maine to California." The table is divided into small squares numbered, and the players stake their money on the numbers of their choice. A weazen old Mexican, with palsied form, drops ten cents on the ace; a boy not more than thirteen ventures on the tray, and some soldiers fill other spaces of the board. "Are you all down—all done?" The dice-box is rattled, and the little ivory bits are rolled out. The old Mexican trembles, and his sunken eyes glisten as if a fortune depended on the result, whereas it is only bread. No ace is turned up on the dice, and he loses; so does the boy; but the soldiers win and "go in" again. The other tables are occupied by Spanish monte and faro, and each attracts crowds of spectators and customers. There is another gambling-house, on a more extensive scale, a little farther up the street, and a dance-house a little way below. The Mexican *baile* is a very well-conducted affair, and the señoritas who attend them give no hint of their actual levity in their behavior. The music and movements of the waltzes are sometimes very novel and pretty, but the *baile* is, after all, but a common dance, leading to immoral purposes.

I can not begin to catalogue all the vices of Santa Fé, for it is probably the fastest little city in the world. In such a city—with a population gathered from all quarters—where most of the sojourners are big-coated, broad-shouldered miners, stock-raisers, and soldiers, fresh from confinement in solitary ranches or long marches over the Plains, and seeking an outlet for a six-months' accumulation of pent-up deviltry—it would be strange if there were not a good deal of wickedness on the surface. But besides these rough-and-

tumble elements there is a small—very small—
coterie of prosperous merchants and professional
men of responsibility; and even these do not
incur any discredit by frequenting the common
dance-house or sitting down in a public place
and staking their money on the faro table. It
is here the most serious objection to Santa Fé
comes in. Some recklessness and dissipation is
inevitable in all growing Western towns, but
the moral sentiment of a place is at a very low
ebb indeed when the husbands of decent women and the fathers of innocent children are
conscious of no disgrace in exposing their love
for such degraded amusements. A room in the
principal hotel is devoted to gambling, and no
secrecy is made of the fact. The prominent mer-
chant with a spare hour on his hands wastes it
here, while the clerk dispels his midday languor
by throwing away his dimes on the democratic
chuck-a-luck table a few doors away. "Nothing
is thought of it." You are told this again and
again ; and whenever a breach of propriety is
noticed in society, this is the invariable response.

CHAPTER XII.

A SPECIAL CORRESPONDENT INVALIDED.

The Dangers of the Arroyas—An Unusual Telegraph Line—A Church Three Centuries Old—The Sanguinary Feuds of the Mexicans and Indians—An Attack of Mountain Fever—Sixty Miles for Medicine.

ON the morning we left Santa Fé the weather was clear and warm, and the sky was a beautiful sapphire, with masses of immaculate white floating gently athwart it. A golden haze lay on the mountains. The people were dressed in cool linens and duck, and straw hats. The silver thread in the thermometer stretched itself into the eighties. It was an indolent, dreamy, enervating bit of summer that had fallen into the autumn. We left the town by the stage road to Pueblo, passed the old adobe church that is crumbling to ruin under the weight of two hundred and fifty years, and soon went out among the interminable cacti and pines again. By and by a breeze sprang up, the fleece was blown away, and leaden clouds mantled the sky in its place. We had started out in trousers and shirts. Heavy Ulsters and cavalry overcoats did not avail against the midwinter cold that now crept down upon us from the mountains and chilled the stoutest of us to the marrow. The clouds thickened and lowered, and the lightning broke in forks and spirals against somber peaks. Then the rain came down in a flood and drenched us to the skin; having succeeded in which, it changed to a spiteful hail, and beat against us until our faces and hands tingled with pain. Now, you may think that such a sudden change of weather is phenomenal, as it would be elsewhere; but in the neighborhood of Santa Fé it is quite common, and the inhabitants are so used to it that, it is facetiously said, they never venture out in a light suit without carrying an Esquimaux overcoat over their arm and a seal-skin cap in their pockets.

I went along the road with a little stream of water mournfully trickling from the brim of my hat down on my nose, and my clothes clinging to me like a worn-out mustard-plaster, envying with all my heart the author of "A Princess of Thule," and "The Strange Adventures of a Phaeton," the only man known to me who is gifted with the happy power of thoroughly enjoying a rain-storm, and the singular equanimity of disposition that enables him to discover beauties out of a wet jacket. No doubt he would have seen all the elements of the picturesque in the sloppy road, in the pines with the rain-drops pendent to their spears, in the corn-fields that look so very bright and yellow, in the mysteries that the clouds wove about the hills, in the cheerless gray light, and in the quiet, melancholy spirit that settled on the country with the storm. This cheerfully aquatic person would have become enthusiastic over the brilliantly red mesa bluffs, which, as a stray sunbeam stole out of the clouds, caught the light and reflected it like a mirror. He would have been as content, perchance, with the mist and its play as with a sunny day of warmth and flowers. But nature has not been so kind with us, and rain and cold are unmitigated abominations which steal away the charm of the prettiest scenery. Speak of the gray light and the mystic haze to more romantic people, and let us have the shelter of a sound tent and three pairs of double blankets.

The country which the stage-coach traverses is settled with numerous ranches, and is one of the most fertile parts of the Territory. The houses are mostly built of logs, which are far better than adobe. I fancy there is a vigor and honesty about them that adapt them for the ideal home of a pioneer. The adobes always seem groveling and effete to me; but the rough little cabins built of sinews of pine are monuments of enterprise, hardihood, and determination.

We made camp at seven o'clock in the evening. The rain was still falling, and the air was bitterly cold. Every dish on our little supper table was flooded, and all through the night the storm beat against our tents, and the waters roared in an adjacent arroya.

The arroyas, by the way, are one of the many peculiar features of Colorado, Arizona, and New Mexico. They are sandy channels, from five to a hundred feet deep, running through the land, with vertical sides. They are usually quite dry, but in a rain-storm they are filled with wild, foaming streams that sweep down without any premonition in an immense volume. I have seen one of them without a drop of water in it at the beginning of a storm, and before many minutes have elapsed there has been a terrific roar, and a flood has rushed down with a straight wall five or six feet deep. Frequently accidents occur to inexperienced travelers who camp in their treacherous shelter, and many lives and much valuable property have been lost in their precipitous floods.

A telegraph line connecting Santa Fé and Pueblo spans the road, but it is so often out of order that it is almost useless. It was built by the Western Union Company, and proved so unprofitable that they transferred it to the Government, in consideration of the privilege of sending all their messages free. Its maintenance costs about $12,000 a month, and it is in working order on about three days out of the seven. A reward is offered for the capture of any person found damaging the line, but the line is damaged every week, and the offender is never brought to justice. When a teamster breaks the tongue of his wagon, or can not conveniently find wood for his fire, he tears down a telegraph pole. The shaft of a stage-coach was broken, and the unfortunate "singing wire" came to grief again. The day we left Santa Fé the line was in order for the first time in a week. The following morning we met a repairer hurrying along the road, who greeted us in the polite manner common to Americans in the Territory—"Say! have you fellows seen the line down anywheres?" We had not, and he continued on his way after telling us that "the —— thing was broke again." The operator at Santa Fé leads a splendidly idle life, and, tilted in an easy chair, absorbs himself in an all-day-long contemplation of his boots, while the little Morse instrument on the desk is as silent as its immortal inventor.

On the third day out from Santa Fé we reached Koslowsky's ranch, which is near Rio Pecos and within a mile of the ruins of a church at least three hundred years old. This weather-beaten old sanctuary is a conspicuous object in the surrounding landscape, bounded by high hills and stratified mesas; and at sunset, when its broken walls of red adobe are touched by the glow, it looks very pretty and romantic. It is cruciform in shape, and is about one hundred feet long. The roof has gone, but the other parts, especially the woodwork, which is finely carved, are in an excellent state of preservation. The walls are six feet thick in many places, and yet it is surprising, considering their friable substance, that the storms of three centuries, with hail and rain, have not succeeded in dissolving them. There is a tradition that the church was once the scene of a great massacre; that some Mexican adventurers, who desired to penetrate the interior of the Territory, were opposed by the Indians; that the savages were invited to a conference in the church; that, attending, they were all assaulted and slaughtered by the Mexicans, and that the chancel was flooded by their blood. The legend is very simple and straightforward, and sounds veracious, though I would not dare to vouch that it is not of the stuff that is woven out of fireside gossip and grandfathers' stories.

From Koslowsky's we struck across the country to Galisteo, and here the writer ignominiously broke down under a severe attack of chills and fever. I was unable to travel farther: I was delirious and exhausted, and was left at the ranch of an American, with the understanding that the party would return for me in three weeks, during which time they were to be occupied in the Placer Mountains. The reader probably has no idea what it is to be ill in a southwestern Mexican town—how utterly the patient despairs, and how homesick he becomes. Galisteo was then about three hundred and fifty miles from the railway (it is nearer now), and, judged by Sydney Smith's standard, it was sixty times that far from a lemon. It consists of a small collection of mud houses and a population of about five hundred. The only American resident was my host, a native of Massachusetts, who emigrated to the Territory twenty-one years ago and married a Mexican woman. He tried to be kind, but his rough attentions could not alleviate the desolation of the dark and dreary days of my sickness. There was a baby in the family who was petulantly and perpetually vocal from sunrise to sunset. A very small negress, with a most extraordinary head of erectile hair, was dedicated to this sweet infant, and paraded him with a singular guttural noise which either gave him great solace or abashed him by showing him the feebleness of his own puerile efforts. At all events, as long as the guttural noise was continued he was comparatively quiet, but the moment it ceased he renewed his bellowings. In the evening, when the baby was taken out of hearing, the dogs began an exasperating concert, which was continued till daybreak. There were about thirteen attached to the house—large mastiffs, with mouths that could comfortably accommodate a man's thigh, and small curs with preternaturally long bodies and short legs. I had an affection for dogs once; now I longed to tickle their appetites with arsenic.

On the third day of my stay I became so much worse that I decided to go into Santa Fé for medicines by a wagon that was to return the following afternoon. The following afternoon was wet and cold, the driver was drunk, and we did not start on the homeward journey until about five o'clock. It was then raining hard, and it soon became so dark that it was impossible to keep the road. We went plunging across the country in a wild, haphazard fashion, rolling down arroyas and striking trees, until about nine at night, when we saw the welcome fire of a Mexican hay-camp, reaching which we pulled up for the night. My teeth were playing a death-like tattoo, and my overcoat and inner garments were wet through. The rain continued to fall heavily, and the fire was soon quenched. Oh, most unhappy night! The wagon was uncovered and afforded no shelter. Only two things were possible: I could either keep my blood in circulation by walking about, or I could lie on the sloppy ground and try to sleep. I kept a lonely patrol until about midnight, and then sank down from sheer exhaustion. Daylight never brought more joy with it than it did when I saw the blackness turning to gray in the east, and a rift in the gray revealing a crimson blush in the overcast sky. Our driver harnessed the horses again, and we jolted off along the deeply rutted road toward Galisteo, where we arrived about noon. My illness continued for several weeks; but by slow degrees strength came back to me, after an experience of misery that excites the greatest self-commiseration when I think of it.

Leaving Galisteo after my recovery, in a southeasterly direction, our party crossed a country furrowed by gigantic mesas, flanked by sheer bluffs a thousand feet high. From the summit of these table-lands the eye explores in every direction, and follows for scores of miles the unbroken ridges that look like clouds drawn across the clear blue sky. They are not comparable with anything in the Eastern or Middle States, and give New Mexico a peculiarly strange and never-to-be-forgotten aspect. The bluffs are mostly of yellow sandstone, lying in rough strata or transverse tablets about the thickness of the flags used in a city sidewalk. The yellow is sometimes streaked with white, and it has a golden shimmer in the sunlight, which toward evening inflames it with crimson. The loose rocks are studded with dwarf spruce or pine, set far apart. Occasionally they remind one of a piece of yellow old Dresden china by their creamy color, with the dots of dull green; but they are so entirely unique that no compact simile is adequate to give an idea of them. Toward sunset, when you look through their long channels on to the silent waves of the plains that engirth them, and see the night drifting in from the East like the smoke of a distant city, and the broad flashes of light falling on the short yellow grass, their lower walls are steeped in a deep blue, while their upper strata blaze with red and orange colors as the warm rays of the sun touch them. But usually it is only under such brilliant effects of atmosphere and light that the mesas have a pleasant appearance to the common eye. At other times their arid, verdureless abutments, and harsh unsymmetrical outlines, tend to produce a sense of waste and rudeness, and opposite feelings to those inspired by the more familiar phases of nature.

CHAPTER XIII.

AN EVENTFUL STAGE-COACH JOURNEY.

Primitive Agriculture—How the Writer "Fixed" the Conductor—Three Texan Stockmen on a Carouse—The Beauties of Fisher's Peak—The Expedition seen through the Smoke of a Cigar.

THE branches of the Atchison, Topeka, and Santa Fé, and of the Kansas Pacific Railway, are reaching out toward Santa Fé, and will soon penetrate that ancient city; but in 1875 the terminus of both roads was at Las Animas, a distance of three hundred miles, and passenger communication was maintained by a line of coaches, the fare by which was sixty dollars, or twenty cents a mile; this including only fifty pounds of baggage. Express matter was charged for at the rate of about twenty-two cents a pound, and as that rate was to some extent prohibitory, the common freight was transported from the railroad to the interior by ox-teams that consumed weeks on the way. No one need be told what the consequences of this inadequacy are. There is scarcely a piece of mechanism of any kind in the Territory, for the reason that unless a duplicate of every rivet and rod is kept on hand, a break-down renders the machine useless for the months that must elapse while duplicates are being obtained from the States. A Buckeye mower is as great a curiosity to the average native as a chapter of Arabic would be; and threshing machines are substituted by a process that would have reflected little credit on the economy or ingenuity of ten centuries ago. The threshing is done on a floor of adobe in a circular stockade of unhewn logs inserted vertically in the ground. The wheat is heaped in the center of this, and the cattle are then driven in to trample the grain from the chaff. Sometimes, from either indolence or carelessness, the stockade is dispensed with, and I have seen five adult persons fully occupied in reducing a small stack of wheat by driving a flock of sheep around its edges.

When our work took us over the road, the sight of the lumbering old stage rolling along at a dead-alive pace, with four unhappy passengers cooped up inside, invariably filled me with dread;

for I remembered that I too would have to submit to the torture. But my anticipations were far exceeded in misery by the realization. The members of the expedition were engaged for three weeks in the country south of Las Vegas ; and here I left them to return East, making the journey to the railway at Las Animas by the Santa Fé coach, which passed through the town at five o'clock in the morning. Thirty minutes before that hour, on a cold, dark morning, I stood under the portico of Chapman's ranch and hotel, quite uncertain as to whether I should be able to get a seat or not. Sometimes, I was told, the coach came in empty, sometimes it was full. In the latter case, I could either wait until the following day, or ride in the "boot." If it was full again the next day, I still would have to wait, and there seemed to be a sickening possibility that I might become old and gray in waiting at Las Vegas. But abuses of the Southern Overland Mail and Express Company had filled the traveling community with such a degree of terror that their vehicles were not usually overcrowded with passengers, and their principal emolument accrued from a postal subsidy, which, although reduced from over one hundred thousand dollars per annum to thirty thousand, still yielded a handsome profit. At all events, the coach arrived from Santa Fé empty, and I prepared to follow the directions given me for making myself as comfortable as possible. In the first place, I was told to bribe the conductor with sundry drinks to take the seats from the inside to the outside, so as to leave me plenty of room; secondly, to bribe the driver with more drinks not to "peach" on the conductor; and thirdly, to bribe one of the station-masters to strew an extra quantity of hay — for my ease in reclining—on the bottom of the coach. With all the trepidation of a guilty conscience I did this disgraceful work of corruption, and watched the whisky gurgling down the three bronzed throats with irresistible admiration for the constitutions that could endure it. I was in such a nervous hurry to "fix things" that I forgot to speak of the favors I wanted until I had paid the barkeeper, when the conductor, wiping his mouth with the back of his hand, stuttered, "Just full." Had the remark referred to his bibulous capacity, it would have been very appropriate; but after gulping some ice-water, which was in the same proportion to the spirits as Falstaff's pennyworth of bread to the gallons of sack scored to him, he continued, "Four of you will just balance her." I found that three burly Texan stockmen, red-eyed, sallow, and sleepy-looking after last night's debauch, were to be my fellow-passengers in the miserable journey of fifty-three hours before me; and with many misgivings I entered the coach and squeezed myself into a seat.

The reader probably has no idea of how jovial a ruffian a Texan stockman is—how infinite his profanity, how broad his sense of humor. His coat-tail of sensibilities is always in the way of discussion, and the foot that treads on it has the disastrous effect of a hammer striking a can of nitro-glycerine.

Two of my companions were stupid and sleepy when we started, but the constant jolt of the coach kept them half awake and swearing. The third occupied himself in dressing an ugly pistol-wound in the abdomen, which he proudly exhibited to me as the memorial of a recent combat near the border of old Mexico. As the sun rose, however, two bottles were produced from under the seat, and then—well, I sincerely hope that I may be spared a repetition of the same experience. In two hours the bottles were tossed out of the window after having been passed from hand to hand until they were drained to a drop; and in inverse ratio to the depression of the contents, the spirits of the men increased in buoyancy, until their exuberance was terrible to behold. The conductor looked in and grinned, while I crouched into a corner, apprehensively watching the elephantine play which threatened to crush me every moment. I protested and entreated in vain.

"Bill, this yar fellow objects," hiccoughed one of the men to his mates.

"All right," readily responded Bill; "chuck him out of the winder!"

The big-booted ruffians hugged, bit, and rolled over each other in wild glee; and as we jolted over the hillocks they bounced to the roof and came down like lumps of lead. In the course of a few hours they partly subsided, however, and dropped down into the bottom of the coach. Even their stomachs were not proof against the combined effects of Las Vegas whisky and the oscillation of the coach. Their faces whitened to a deathly hue, and the smiles waned into the idiotic vacancy of drunkenness. One of them struggled up to the window and put his head out—for what purpose I can only guess; and when we sat down again he hiccoughed: "Never in a cosh in in all my life that wasn't sea-shick," afterward relapsing into his former state of silent imbecility. The others lay huddled together in the most agonizing of positions, with their heads bent on their chests and their limbs doubled under them, all unconscious of suffering, in a befuddled sleep. The day went on drearily as we rolled through some of the least interesting country I had yet seen — everlasting reaches of plain, a dull yellow in color, like a corn-field after harvest, and frequently upraised into the curious hills called "hogbacks," which are approached by an easy acclivity on one side, and on the other side present a sheer rocky front. At stations from six to ten miles apart we obtained relays of horses, although our speed never exceeded four miles an hour, and it occasionally dwindled down to two. The road was atrociously bad, and the coach seemed to leap into the air, so severe was the jolting.

For the greater part of the first day's ride my companions were insensible, but toward evening they revived and climbed out through the windows on to the roof, so that I spent one quiet hour alone in comparative comfort. The coach was about the size of a *coupée*, with two benches, six inches wide and three and a half feet long, stretched athwart. It was covered with canvas, and was without glass windows, the substitutes for them being blinds fastened with a buckle and strap. The bottom was strewn with dirt and hay —principally dirt—and the seats were covered with leather. These accommodations were intended for four passengers, and by dint of much squeezing that number could seat themselves; but the prospect of confinement in this narrow space for more than two days and two nights was beyond endurance. Sleep was impossible, and when we were packed up for the night, and I was wedged in between the besotted stockmen, with my arms and legs bound to one position—when the cold wind swept in through the many crevices, and my head ached and eyes were heavy— I prayed that Heaven would not forget Barlow, Sanderson & Co. Many are the sins you will answer for, unkindest and most extortionate of Jehus! Many the headaches, many the sleepless hours, great the hunger you have caused your unoffending and liberal patrons! On the first day we had breakfast at 9 o'clock, consisting of buffalo meat, eggs, and bread. The next meal was at 8 in the evening, consisting of fried pork, bread, and coffee. At 5 in the morning on the second day, a negro appeared at the coach-door with the inquiry: "Say, you fell's! want any breakfast heah?" A heavy boot was thrust into his face, and accompanied with a jocular request that he should go to ——. I scarce closed my eyes during the long night. How the coach held together in the concussions it was subjected to was a puzzle which I pondered over until I dozed, and a more violent shock than ever restored me to wakefulness.

On the morning of the second day we crossed the Rocky Mountains by the Raton Pass, with its romantic scenery, and came in sight of Fisher's Peak, a truncated cone, glowing with the warm colors of autumn foliage. It resembles an enormous tumulus rather than a natural formation, and its successive terraces are ribbed with deeply colored rock. Its northern front extends to the southeast in a long line of cliffs, so even on the edge that they suggest a wall artificially built for the protection of the thriving little town, with its straggling streets and rude wooden buildings, that lies to the north. We had left the adobes of

New Mexico behind, and in Trinidad, Colorado, we saw the activity and promise of a well-to-do frontier settlement. Even in the Mexican towns where Americans are settled, the dead weight of the people's heritage of oppression, ignorance, and vice obstructs enterprise and is felt in a pervading atmosphere of decay. The best friends of the Territory acknowledge that its progress will be retarded until the Mexicans are superseded by immigrants of a more energetic and moral character.

At Trinidad the roads to Pueblo and Las Animas met, and the passengers to the latter place were transferred to another and yet smaller coach. The stockmen contemplated "lying over," but they eventually decided to continue the journey, and another passenger was added to our number— a small, fussy, talkative Methodist preacher. He rode with the driver during the afternoon, when the beautiful Spanish Peaks and the glorious old Pike's were in views—the latter looming up more than a hundred miles, as prominently as when I first saw it from the Union Pacific Railway five months before—but in the evening he came inside and wedged himself into a corner. The Texans had lost their spirits, or they would probably have thrown him out of the window; but instead of that they determined to smoke him out on to the box again. They filled the foulest of pipes with the vilest of tobacco, and puffed thick clouds into his face. They swore the roundest of oaths and sang the vilest of songs. The poor old gentleman coughed a mild protest, and complained that some of the songs, which would have shocked the audience of a Water Street dance-house, were "a little coarse." He was as determined to be amiable and conciliatory as his tormentors were determined to be mischievous ; but they would not desist, and when the coach stopped at midnight for supper, the only meal we had in thirteen hours, he resumed his seat on the box and retained it throughout the bitterly cold night. We were detained an hour while supper was being cooked in the log-house before which we had pulled up, and were supplied with eggs and beefsteak at the usual price of a dollar a head. Another sleepless night went by, and at ten o'clock on the next morning we arrived at Las Animas. I took great pains to find out on which road the stockmen intended to travel ; and succeeding, I resisted their kind invitations to travel with them, and bought a ticket by the other line.

Forty-eight hours later I sat down in the Palmer House to a pint of Chateau La Rose and a tenderloin à la Russe ; and afterward, as a soft Cabaña lent its flavor to the retrospect, my experiences in the saddle, the tedious marches, and the frugal mess, seemed so pleasant that I resolved to repeat them the following year.

THE END.

www.ingramcontent.com/pod-product-compliance
Lightning Source LLC
Chambersburg PA
CBHW030242170426
43202CB00009B/596